John Maynard Keynes

Columbia Essays on the Great Economists
Donald J. Dewey, General Editor

◄►◄►◄►

John Maynard
KEYNES

◄►◄►◄►

by Hyman P. Minsky

COLUMBIA UNIVERSITY PRESS NEW YORK

Hyman P. Minsky is a Professor of Economics
at Washington University, St. Louis, Missouri.

Copyright © 1975 Columbia University Press
Printed in the United States of America

Library of Congress Cataloging in Publication Data

Minsky, Hyman P
    John Maynard Keynes.

    (Great economists series)
    Bibliography: p. 171
1. Keynes, John Maynard, 1883-1946. The general theory of employment,
    interest, and money. 2.   Keynesian economics.   I.   Series.
        HB99.7.K38M55   330.15'6   75-17900
                ISBN 0-231-03616-7
                ISBN 0-231-03917-4 pbk.
                10 9 8 7 6 5 4 3 2

Preface

John Maynard Keynes's special status rests upon his "revolutionary" work, *The General Theory of Employment, Interest, and Money*. This study focuses upon that work and the claim that it revolutionized economic thought: the theme is that *The General Theory* does embody a revolutionary change in economic theory, but that in the process of arriving at today's standard version of what Keynes was about the revolution was aborted. Thus an attempt is made to recover the revolutionary thrust of *The General Theory*.

This book concentrates on *The General Theory* and virtually ignores the substantial body of Keynes's earlier work on monetary theory. The huge literature that developed, explained, interpreted, and formalized Keynes is also virtually ignored. The reason for these omissions is not that I deem Keynes's prior work or the literature to be unimportant, but because a thorough, documented study of Keynes's work and the discussion it triggered would get in the way of my message, which is that in the neglected facets of *The General Theory* there is a theory of the processes of a capitalist economy that is much more appropriate for problems of economic analysis and policy now confronting us than is contained in the standard economic theory.

The interpretation of Keynes put forth here evolved over a number of years. One input was my work on financial instability. Another input was the work of economists who, each in his own way, took issue with the standard interpretation: Joan Robinson, G. L. S. Schackle, Nicholas Kaldor, Sidney Weintraub, Paul Davidson, Robert Clower, and Axel Leijonhufvud are prominent among the dissidents who affected my thinking. It would take a far longer volume than this for me to detail points of agreement and disagreement with those colleagues in dissent, and such disputation and detailing of views would interfere with the message I want to send.

A further input into the evolution of my views was discussions I had during a most pleasant sabbatical year in Cambridge. In particular I want to thank Donald Moggridge, who at the time was beginning to delve into the Keynes papers to prepare what has since appeared as Volume XIII *(The General Theory and After: Part I, Preparation)* and Volume XIV *(The General Theory and After: Part II, Defence and Developement)* of *The Collected Works of John Maynard Keynes,* for some very good talks. However in this work, the material in Volume XIII and XIV is not taken into account explicitly. My manuscript was at the publishers by the time these volumes appeared. Furthermore, any detailed examination of this material is the subject matter of a quite different sort of book.

In addition to Donald Moggridge, I want to thank Professors Joan Robinson and W. B. Reddaway as well as Aubrey Silberston and Alan Roe for bearing with me while I was in Cambridge. I owe very much to the perceptive comments and criticisms of Phyllis Freeman, Laurence H. Meyer, Maurice Townsend, and Bernard Shull. None of the above are responsible for the errors and misinterpretations which may follow.

I want to thank the Social Science Research Council, the National Science Foundation, and of course my home base, Washington University, for support in this endeavor. They, too, are not responsible for what follows. Ms. Connie Pritchard was rapid, efficient, and conscientious in the typing and clerical support; Ms. Susan Shiff very efficiently took over the checking of galleys and prepared the index. Bernard Gronert and Karen Mitchell of Columbia University Press were both patient and helpful.

For permission to quote extensively from *The General Theory of Employment, Interest and Money,* by John Maynard Keynes, thanks are due to Harcourt Brace Jovanovich, Inc. and The Royal Economic Society.

A special thanks goes to my wife Esther, who aided and abetted this work in many quiet ways.

Hyman P. Minsky
June 1975

Introduction

There are times in the intellectual history of a discipline
when its theoretical house is in good order; at other times this house is in
disarray. When the house is in good order there is a broad consensus
about its content and it seems to yield useful results, both in interpreting
observations and as a guide to policy or technology. When the theoretical
house is in disarray, qualified practitioners disagree about the contents:
there are competing theories, and for every competing theory there exist
observations which are difficult to explain. Every theory seems to be of
limited usefulness; anomalies abound.

A few years ago—in the early to mid-1960s—macroeconomics and
monetary theory appeared to comprise a well-behaved and mature discipline. At that time, in spite of the existence of various mavericks and
deviants, which seems to be unavoidable in the social disciplines, most
professional economists seemed to agree that the neoclassical synthesis,
which integrated the innovations of Keynes with the apparatus and results of the classical tradition, was the appropriate framework to guide
both theoretical and empirical research, as well as economic policy
analysis and prescription. Today, in good part because policy failures,
acting as proxies for critical experiments, revealed shortcomings in the

analytical foundations, macroeconomic and monetary theory are in disarray.

The last paragraph of Keynes's most famous work, *The General Theory of Employment, Interest and Money*, contains the oft-cited passage: "ideas of economists and political philosophers, both when they are right and when they are wrong, are more powerful than is commonly understood. Indeed the world is ruled by little else" (*GT*, p. 383). In the sentence preceding the above Keynes noted: "At the present moment people are unusually expectant of a more fundamental diagnosis; more particularly ready to receive it, eager to try it out, if it should be even plausible" (*GT*, p. 383).

At this writing the mood in the United States is similar to that Keynes described. Even without the proximate cause of a great worldwide depression, but perhaps because of the persistence of inflation, the awareness of poverty not only in the midst of plenty but also because of plenty, the renewed experience and fear of financial instability, and the unsettled conditions of international trade and finance, there is a gnawing dissatisfaction with the state of both the economy and economic thought and a growing disenchantment with the policy measures that have been adopted to affect the economy. It follows that the theoretical framework which, when applied, indicated that these policy choices were apt requires reexamination.

Thus, in the 1970s the climate apparently is ripe for another "intellectual revolution" like the one *The General Theory* triggered in the 1930s.

In this book, which interprets Keynes's major contribution to economics, I contend that the ingredients for such a "second revolution" in our way of thinking about advanced capitalism exist in some neglected facets and logical extensions of the argument that Keynes advanced in *The General Theory*. My view is that what became popular and was accepted into the fold of conventional economics is but a part of the substance of Keynes's argument. Those ideas were accepted which both were most easily assimilated into the body of the older ideas—what Keynes called classical economics—and had the greatest relevance to the immediate problems facing the world in the late 1930s and early 1940s: the stagnant aftermath of the Great Depression and the mobilization for and waging of the Second World War. I also hold that what has been neglected or lost is a major part of the substance of *The General Theory*; this lost portion makes a sharp break with the formulations fundamental to the older classical doctrines and is more immediately relevant to problems the advanced economies are now facing. Thus the integrated Keynesian classical economic theory—what is labeled the neoclassical synthesis—does violence to both the spirit and the substance of Keynes's work.

The substance of what was neglected in the development of the synthesis can be grouped under three headings: decision-making under uncertainty, the cyclical character of the capitalist process, and financial relations of an advanced capitalist economy. In the neoclassical synthesis Keynes's emphasis upon disequilibrium, i.e., upon "the fact that it is in the transition [among never-attained positions of equilibrium] that we actually have our being" (*GT*, p. 343), is ignored. The models of the neoclassical synthesis are essentially timeless, whereas Keynes in *The General Theory* was always conscious of time, process, and the transitory nature of particular situations. Furthermore, while *The General Theory* quite explicitly dealt with an economy with particular institutional characteristics, the standard interpretation abstracts from institutional detail. In particular, in the various versions of the neoclassical synthesis the financial mechanism, which is central to Keynes's interests, is almost always treated in a most truncated fashion.

Once the usually neglected aspects of the argument of *The General Theory* are taken into account, a model of the capitalist process emerges which is more useful in explaining the behavior of American and other advanced capitalist economies in boom, recession, and inflationary high-level stagnation, and more relevant for determining policy than is today's conventional theory. As reinterpreted here, Keynes challenges the dominance in our economic thinking of the basic constructs of the neoclassical system—the production function and invariant preference systems—and so opens the door to serious policy proposals addressing the "what kind" and "for whom" questions so important today.

Keynes's theory as conventionally interpreted legitimized the use of monetary and fiscal policy instruments to attain full employment; such policy is now quite orthodox. Standard economic theory tells us that the kind of output and the distribution of this output are determined by the fundamental production and preference characteristics of the economy. The perspective derived from the alternative interpretation of Keynes enables us to go beyond a generalized full-employment policy and turns the question of what kind of employment and how (to whom) income is distributed into a policy decision. Once again, the dimensions of legitimate policy are broadened.

Within the argument of *The General Theory* a number of different threads can be discerned. Some threads lead back to the older classical theory and reflect Keynes's failure to fully escape from the "habitual modes of thought and expression," (*GT*, p. viii) of which he warned. Other threads lead to a successful escape from the old ideas. Keynes never clearly differentiated between the threads. In only one instance, his rebuttal to Professor Viner's review (which is central to our argument), did he publicly discuss the validity of an interpretation of his book. Viner's review tied Keynes's new theory into the old, and Keynes quite explicitly denied the validity of Viner's interpretation. Other interpretations, which looked back to the old, were either ignored or casually accepted by Keynes. As a result of this neglect to repudiate the standard interpretation, which ties Keynes into the classical doctrines he believed he was replacing, the standard interpretation has some claim to legitimacy. However, these perhaps legitimate offspring did not inherit these attributes of *The General Theory* that reflected Keynes's success in escaping from the confines of the orthodox economic theory, attributes which point to an alternative way of looking at an advanced capitalist economy.

Because of my emphasis upon the new in *The General Theory*, I will virtually ignore Keynes's extensive writings as an economist prior to *The General Theory*. (However in delineating the social philosophy and public policy implications of *The General Theory*, I will show that the implications Keynes drew were clearly consistent with the public-policy views he held in the 1920s.) I will also neglect other dimensions of his many-faceted career. My focus is narrow: it is upon *The General Theory of Employment, Interest and Money* as an effort to revolutionize economics.

In what follows I will argue, as Keynes did in *The General Theory*, as if we are dealing with a closed economy. Obviously, in the applications of the theory—whether standard or reinterpreted—allowance must be made for international impacts and feedbacks. In particular, in my reinterpretation of Keynes, financial relations, disturbances, and instability play a major role in the successions of systems states that characterize the path of the economy. In the light of the evidence of the 1960s and the early 1970s it is clear that in the semi-open system that rules among the advanced capitalist economies, the significance of financial disturbances and instability is if anything greater than if each of these economies were treated in isolation. Thus the phrasing of the argument, which treats financial systems as if they related to closed economies, is a matter of expository convenience and necessity. The essence of a cyclical and financial-instability interpretation of Keynes can be presented within this framework, and the opening up of the domain of interest to a system of interrelated open capitalist economies can only reinforce, not attenuate, the strength of this argument.

Contents

John Maynard Keynes

‹1›

The General Theory and its Interpretation

If Keynes, along with Marx, Darwin, Freud, and Einstein, belongs in the pantheon of seminal thinkers who triggered modern intellectual revolutions, it is because of the contribution to economics, both as a science and as a relevant guide to public policy, that is contained in his *General Theory of Employment, Interest and Money*.

This volume was published in February 1936, when Keynes was 52 years old. He first appeared in print as a professional economist in 1909. His first professional article, "Recent Economic Events in India"[1] dealt with the impact upon India of the worldwide depression and financial disturbances of 1907–8, with particular emphasis upon a monetary phenomenon, the mechanism of the rupee issue. From this first article up to 1935 he wrote extensively on economic matters, addressing both professionals and the public, with special emphasis on problems in monetary economics; even his substantial contributions to international economics dealt largely with the financial and monetary aspects.

[1]*Economics Journal*, March 1909.

His work in economics during the twenty-five years prior to 1935, while novel in detail, often subject to controversy, and typically deviating from the conventional wisdom when discussing public policy, was, on the whole, in the discipline's mainstream: his criticisms were within but not of standard theory. A capsule characterization of Keynes's serious contributions to economic theory prior to the appearance of *The General Theory* is that he was mainly concerned with making more precise the manner in which the then standard theory of money—the quantity theory—worked.

The fundamental propositions of the quantity theory of money are that for positions of equilibrium, money is neutral, in the sense that relative prices, incomes, and output do not depend upon the quantity of money; that the general level of prices is determined by the quantity of money; and that a decentralized economy is fundamentally stable. Keynes's attitude, prior to *The General Theory*, was that these quantity-theory propositions were basically valid, but that the theory was vague and imprecise about the mechanisms and processes by which the long-run results were achieved, and that more had to be known about how the economy behaves in between positions of equilibrium—i.e., in the short run, defined as disequilibrium or transitory states—before the theory could be fully accepted.

The General Theory marked a sharp break with this earlier position on the quantity theory. Keynes attacked with gusto and obvious relish the logical and empirical foundations of traditional economics. He redefined the problems of economic theory as the determination of aggregate demand, and thus employment, in the short run, within an analytical framework that explicitly recognized that it was dealing with a capitalist economy subject to booms and crises. He introduced novel tools of analysis, such as the consumption function and liquidity preference, and employed concepts unfamiliar to mainstream economics, such as uncertainty. His analysis yielded the result that money was not neutral. In contrast to the quantity theory, his theory showed that real variables depend in an essential way on monetary and financial variables; that the price level does not depend solely or even mainly on the quantity of money; and that the transitional processes are such that a decentralized, unplanned, capitalist economy—one in which economic policy did not intervene in an appropriate manner—was not a self-correcting system that tended toward a stable equilibrium at full employment. In Keynes's new view full employment, if achieved, was itself a transitory state.

The General Theory burst upon the scene as a well-advertised great work—so advertised by both Keynes and the younger economists at Cambridge and elsewhere who surrounded him. Keynes wrote to George Bernard Shaw: "I believe myself to be writing a book on economic theory which will largely revolutionize . . . the way the world thinks about economic problems."[2] It was accepted as such by many of Keynes's peers and most especially by the younger generation, the then neophyte economists, on both sides of the Atlantic. As Paul M. Sweezy noted in his obituary of Keynes, *The General Theory* produced a "sense of liberation and intellectual stimulus . . . among younger teachers and students in all the leading British and American Universities." Furthermore, Keynes "opened up new vistas and new pathways to a whole generation of economists."[3]

The General Theory was an immediate success. Nevertheless, even since its publication a process of diminishing and denigrating the significance of the contribution has been at work, a process to which both ostensible friends of the new doctrines, such as J. R. Hicks, and overt foes, such as J. Viner, have contributed.

Today the dominant view among professional economists may very well be that the model Keynes discussed is at most an interesting and perhaps intermittently relevant special case, and that generally speaking Keynes did not succeed in replacing the old classical economics with a new Keynesian economics. For example, in the introduction to his successful textbook, *Macroeconomic Theory*, Gardner Ackley, who was first a member (1962–64) and then chairman (1964–68) of the "Keynesian" President's Council of Economic Advisors during the Kennedy-Johnson era, holds "that Keynes' work represents more an extension than a revolution of "Classical" ideas and the tide of post-Keynesian literature has carried macroeconomics far beyond the high-water mark of Keynes' own great contribution."[4]

Ackley's evaluation of Keynes's contribution is not atypical. Many current views leave the impression that the excitement that greeted the

---

[2] Harrod, *The Life of John Maynard Keynes*, p. 642.
[3] Sweezy, "John Maynard Keynes," p. 301.
[4] Ackley, *Macroeconomic Theory*, p. viii.

appearance of *The General Theory* was an error. Today's perspective seems to be that what was valid was not new, and what was new was not valid. Either the present-day interpretation, as exemplified by Ackley, or the interpretation of Keynes's contribution as an intellectual revolution—which was how Sweezy and others greeted the work—is a misinterpretation of the content: both views cannot be valid.

The position taken in this book is that the evaluation by Keynes and his contemporaries—as exemplified by Sweezy—of *The General Theory* as revolutionary is correct; the work does contain the seeds for a deep intellectual revolution in economics and in the economists' view of society. However, these seeds never reached their full fruition. The embryonic scientific revolution was aborted, as the book's ideas were interpreted and analyzed by academics and then applied by these same academics as a guide to public policy.

Even prior to the formal appearance of *The General Theory*, on the basis of Keynes's lectures at Cambridge and circulated galleys, academic economists began to tie the new to the old, the old in monetary theory being the quantity theory of money. The result of the interpretation process has been a well-nigh complete victory for the old in both academic and government circles. The dominant neoclassical synthesis, as exemplified in the work of contemporary American economists such as Samuelson, Patinkin, Modigliani, and Friedman, is more classical than Keynesian; that is, the general or "in principle" validity of the quantity theory of money is upheld. With this victory by the classical theory, academic economics has recaptured much of the sterility and irrelevance with respect to the operation of the real-world economy which characterized the discipline prior to the appearance of *The General Theory*. Patinkin, one of the architects of today's dominant view, celebrated the irrelevance of economic theory when he wrote in the introduction to his influential and prestigious *Money, Interest and Prices* that:

> The propositions of the quantity theory of money hold under conditions much less restrictive than those usually considered necessary by its advocates and, *a fortiori*, its critics. Conversely, the propositions of Keynesian monetary theory are much less general than *The General Theory* . . . and later expositions would lead us to believe. But this in no way diminished the relevance of Keynesian unemployment theory for the formulation of a practicable full employment policy.[5]

[5] Patinkin, *Money, Interest, and Prices: an Integration of Monetary and Value Theory*, p. xxv.

The immediate success of *The General Theory* in the 1930s is attributable to its relevance. When it appeared, the world, and most especially the United States, was in the seventh year of a great depression. In the contemporary chronicles this Great Depression had been triggered by the Wall Street crash of 1929 and reinforced by sundry other financial traumas and crises. The climactic event was the breakdown of the American banking system in the spring of 1933 as Franklin Roosevelt was succeeding Herbert Hoover to the presidency.

During the years of anguish between 1929 and the appearance of *The General Theory*, the dominant orthodox academic economists had little to offer in the way of politically palatable suggestions for an active public policy. The orthodox economists believed in the self-correcting properties of the market mechanism. Thus dominant orthodoxy held that recovery would take place in good time, unless inappropriate policy, which included fiscal intervention, aggravated the situation.

There were economists who though orthodox in their theory were offering policy advice in the early thirties that deviated from the conventional. Throughout the late 1920s, when Britian was experiencing chronic unemployment, Keynes was unorthodox in his policy advice: he supported Lloyd George in the 1929 general election in advocating debt-financed public works to ameliorate unemployment. However, his analysis of the effects of public works was muddled. It is a fine example of apt policy advice that was not based upon a consistent theoretical underpinning.[6]

In the United States, during the era of the Great Depression, the most important group of academic economists offering advice that deviated from the norm centered around the University of Chicago. These economists argued, during the depths of the Great Depression, for what would now be called expansionary monetary and fiscal policy. However, their policy position was not integrated into a theoretical formulation of the capitalist process that explained how the phenomena that policy was to correct resulted from system characteristics.

In the writings of the most persuasive economist in this group, Henry L. Simons of Chicago,[7] the flaws in the American economy that led to the Great Depression were seen as mainly due to institutional weak-

[6]Keynes, "Can Lloyd George Do It?" pp. 86–125.
[7]Simons, *Economic Policy for a Free Society*.

nesses in the banking system and human errors by the authorities rather than systemic, essential characteristics of a capitalist economy. As it is always possible after the event of a crash or a crisis to impute what went wrong to some human error or institutional flaw, the Simons position is essentially irrefutable. As a result of the traditional nature of the theoretical model from which Simons argued, his policy prescriptions, though moving in the appropriate direction from the perspective of the later Keynesian theory, were not conclusions derived from a systematic, integrated analytical formulation. Simons and others like him were guided to appropriate policies more by their intuition and perceptive observations than by their economic theory. Lacking an analytical foundation, Simons' perspective lacked predictive power, and the arguments advanced for the policy prescriptions were not persuasive. Simons was, so to speak, dealing with symptoms rather than the causes of the then seemingly obvious flaws in capitalism.

Even though Franklin Roosevelt was an activist, who wanted to do something to revive the economy, the first phalanx of economic advisors he brought to Washington to serve as house intellectuals were unable to offer him serious, systematic advice on how to go about it. Under their influence Roosevelt undertook a policy of tinkering with the dollar price of gold in an effort to raise prices—especially agricultural prices. It was not until some two or three years later that younger, initially less influential, advisors working in Washington began to advocate, even prior to the appearance of *The General Theory*, the use of fiscal powers to expand the economy. However, this advice did not really affect policy until Roosevelt's second term, and prior to World War II dominant prejudices against spending and deficits were never overcome. Because of the inconsistent thrusts of policy during the first Roosevelt term, the economy, after an initial recovery from the depths of 1932–33, was more depressed than it would have been in the face of consistent expansionist policies. Given the financial trauma of 1929–33, which guaranteed that stagnant and sluggish private spending patterns would prevail for some time, the period 1933–39 was one in which consistent "expansionist" policies both were necessary and would have been most successful.[8]

The major alternative to the traditional economists were the Marxists. Marxist sentiment was strong among the undergraduates and younger

[8]Galbraith, "How Keynes Came to America."

graduates in Cambridge, England, Keynes's intellectual base; after all, *The General Theory* was written during "the red thirties." Orthodox Marxists interpreted the Great Depression as confirming the validity of the view that capitalism is inherently unstable. Thus during the depression's worst days, the mainstream of orthodox economists and the Marxists came to the same policy conclusion: namely, that within a capitalist economy nothing useful could be done to counteract depressions. Whether economists labeled themselves conservative, liberal, or radical, during the 1930s all apparently reached a similar dismal conclusion: within capitalism, depressions took place and ran their course. People and society just had to accommodate themselves to periodic and recurrent hard times.

Ideologically Keynes fit into neither the Marxist nor the traditionalist camp. A product of Edwardian enlightenment and a charter member of the Bloomsbury set, Keynes was naturally skeptical of conventional and authoritative wisdom. Although he was a "man of the left" as that phrase is understood in Europe, it may have been because of his commitment to the professional study of society that he did not go along with the younger Bloomsburies in their drift to the more radical, doctrinaire left in the thirties. Throughout the interwar period, although he was in the establishment, he was not of the various governments. He held a somewhat independent, progressive position; what affiliations and party loyalties he had were to the Liberals. It was out of this mildly left ideological middle ground, and out of an understanding that the Left had the questions but not the answers, that *The General Theory* was born. It may be viewed as the fruit of a union between the hard-headed rationality of a professional economist and a man's commitment to the sentiment that something better than what exists is both possible and attainable.

In *The General Theory* Keynes provided what was both an intellectual and a policy-prescriptive alternative to the dismal views of the traditionalists and the Marxists. His analysis made the events of 1929 and after the result of systemic rather than accidental factors. He shifted the focus of economic analysis from problems of resource allocation to those of the determination of aggregate demand. His new theory allowed for the introduction into the argument of variables which policy can determine. In particular, he defined aggregate demand in such a way that government and private demand were complements when unemployment existed and substitutes at full employment. His system provided an analysis which rationalized the policy thrust which the instincts of activist politicians and liberal intellectuals recommended: that in time of depressions, public works—whether well or inappropriately selected —are conducive to the achievement of full employment. The policy tool which his analysis made legitimate—now called fiscal policy—held out the promise that business cycles, while not avoidable, could be controlled. Keynes provided an alternative to the sterile theorizing and the pessimistic conclusions of both the orthodox and the Marxist economists. He brought economics "back into contact with the real world."[9]

A further factor which led to the immediate, if temporary, acceptance of *The General Theory* as a valid intellectual revolution was that while it marked a break with inherited doctrine, there was in the work and person of Keynes a continuity with traditional economic analysis.

In his major economic publication prior to *The General Theory*, *A Treatise on Money*, Keynes was concerned mainly with determining the dynamic mechanism by which the quantity theory of money operated. The problem he attacked was to determine precisely how changes in the quantity of money worked their way through the economy so that the fundamental theorems of the quantity theory were valid. The inherited quantity theory of money held that in the long run, money is a neutral veil which does not fundamentally affect the operations of the economy; but the inherited theory, not being phrased in terms of short-run processes, never adequately explained why this is so. The paradigm underlying the standard quantity theory is an economy of simple, timeless exchange and production in which transactions among units are by barter. Money is introduced in the standard theory as an efficient device for eliminating the need for a double coincidence of wants to exist in order for trade to take place. Such a double coincidence is necessary if barter is to take place in the absence of specialized trading intermediaries who take positions or hold stocks of commodities. With an abstract concept of money, in a model in which time, durable equipment, and enterprise are introduced in artificial ways, changes in the quantity of money affect only prices; output, employment, and the composition of output are determined in the barter system.

In *A Treatise on Money* Keynes worked with more natural concepts of money than the standard theory admitted, in that money as created by

[9]Sweezy, "John Maynard Keynes," p. 299.

banks indirectly represented business debt. As advanced by Keynes, the short-run mechanism which transmits monetary changes to the price level without fundamentally affecting real variables operates by first affecting business financing of investment. In the first instance, an increase in the quantity of money tends to increase investment being financed and thus the share of investment in output. This increased investment in turn leads to an excess of total demand over supply. As it cannot affect output, this excess demand affects price. Furthermore, once monetary expansion stops, investment falls back to its prior relation to output.

In *The General Theory* Keynes shifts his focus from how money affects investment's share of a fixed output to what in general determines aggregate demand and output. The quantity of money is but one among a number of determinants of aggregate demand. At times changes in money may be ineffective in changing aggregate demand. Until full employment rules, aggregate demand determines the ratio of employed to employable resources. In this way Keynes broadened monetary economics to include fiscal and other determinants of aggregate demand. As a result, monetary economics became macroeconomics. The primary focus was shifted from the determination of the price level to the joint determination of output, employment, and prices.

A major issue in interpreting the nature of Keynes's contribution is whether *The General Theory* is essentially an embellishment, with perhaps a more picturesque and apt set of definitions, of the views embodied in *A Treatise on Money* and other quantity-theory works or whether it marks a distinct break with previous doctrine. The view taken here is that it is a break with the fundamental theoretical posture of *A Treatise on Money*, even though both works deal with processes by which observed phenomena—either prices or output—are determined.

In *A Treatise on Money*, at all times the quantities of output and employment are determined by real factors independent of monetary influences. It is assumed that the market mechanisms of a decentralized capitalist economy will lead to what may be labeled full employment, and that deviations from full employment are transitory and can be imputed to nonessential flaws, such as a poorly conceived Federal Reserve policy or the existence of an unstable banking system.

The view of *The General Theory* is that no such tendency to achieve and then sustain full employment exists; that is, the basic path of a capitalist economy is cyclical.

A Treatise on Money rests upon the determination of system behavior by a theoretical apparatus based upon production functions and simple preference systems. In *The General Theory* this analytical apparatus is discarded—or at least placed in a subordinate position.

In *The General Theory* the speculative nature of asset holding and financing choices dominates production-function characteristics in determining investment output. A fundamental theme of *The General Theory* is that the asset-valuation process is a proximate determinant of investment; Keynes argues that assets, in addition to having characteristics of annuities, may also provide protection by being salable in the event that an uninsurable unfavorable contingency occurs. This marks a fundamental shift of perspective and apparatus from those of the neoclassical view of investment. This shift was obscured, and then ignored, in the process of interpreting the theory. Thus in the modern literature it is not unusual to find studies seeking to determine the parameters of presumably Keynesian investment functions in which production-function assumptions are used to set up the model being subjected to econometric analysis. By their very nature, such studies, based as they are upon erroneous premises, *cannot* determine relevant investment relations. As many things happen together and as econometricians are skilled in massaging data, even such poorly conceived studies may satisfy merely statistical tests of adequacy.

Throughout *A Treatise on Money* Keynes shows an awareness of the complex observations that monetary theory needs to explain. He is aware that it is necessary to replace the mechanical relations of the quantity theory with an analysis of market decisions, linkages, and channels that track what is observed. The attempt to elucidate the process of price-level determination while still maintaining the intellectual framework which rested upon an assumption of barter led Keynes in *A Treatise on Money* as it had led D. H. Robertson in *Banking Policy and The Price Level*,[10] to a complex taxonomy involving many variables, a fine set of definitions, and nice distinctions among variants of the major concepts.

In *The General Theory* Keynes broke the dependence of monetary theory upon classical price theory: monetary phenomena emerged as a full, not a silent, partner in determining system behavior. This enabled

[10]Robertson, *Banking Policy and the Price Level.*

him to connect observations on the behavior of a sophisticated capitalist economy in a clearer, more concise fashion: business cycles were no longer anomalies unexplained by the theory. Once this change of perspective about the significance of money was made, many of the nice distinctions become redundant. Instead of being concerned with many possible paths of the system, the economist had only to deal with a few system states—each state generating a characteristic time series.

A Treatise on Money and *The General Theory* overlap, for they are both attempts to explain much of the same set of observations. Therefore, it is not surprising that many passages in *A Treatise on Money* can be interpreted as foreshadowing *The General Theory*. However, these foreshadowings should not be allowed to obscure the drastic break in concepts and views that is involved.

The General Theory, although concerned with the implications of institutional usage, and quite clearly relevant only to a financially sophisticated capitalist economy, does not contain any detailed description of banking and financial institutions. Such detail is contained in *A Treatise on Money*. In deciding how, if at all, these two major works are to be "synthesized" it is necessary to recognize that the institutional analysis of *A Treatise on Money* served to set out the problems of fianance in a capitalist environment and thus set the background for the theoretical arguments and framework of *The General Theory*. Thus blending the institutional analysis of *A Treatise on Money* with the theory of *The General Theory* seems to be an appropriate way to integrate the two.

Even though the purely Keynesian analysis has been abandoned by today's dominant economic theorists, the primary policy message of Keynes—that slumps are unnecessary and a waste of both human and nonhuman resources—has become a fundamental political axiom guiding economic policy. Although today's mainstream economists differ in the mix of policy instruments they recommend and use different definitions of full employment, there is a common fundamental assertion with respect to economic policy: it is maintained that a proper blend of a limited set of policy instruments assures that full employment, or a close approximation to it, will be achieved.

However, this victory for Keynes's policy objectives and activist policy posture obscures the fact that implicit in his analysis is a view that a capitalist economy is fundamentally flawed. This flaw exists because the financial system necessary for capitalist vitality and vigor—which trans-

lates entrepreneurial animal spirits into effective demand for investment—contains the potential for runaway expansion, powered by an
investment boom. This runaway expansion is brought to a halt because
accumulated financial changes render the financial system fragile, so that
not unusual changes can trigger serious financial difficulties. Because
Keynes arrived at his views on how a capitalist economy operates by
examining problems of decision-making under conditions of intractable
uncertainty, in his system, stability, even if it is the result of policy, is
destabilizing. Even if policy succeeds in eliminating the waste of great
depressions, the fundamental financial attributes of capitalism mean that
periodic difficulties in constraining and then sustaining demand will
ensue. A solution that is explicit in Keynes to the problems arising from
this fundamental instability is to shift the weight of public and private
demand toward the public sectors, so that the potential for evil from the
instability of financial markets and private investment is reduced.

Keynes's great contribution therefore triggered an aborted, or incomplete, revolution in economic thought. His proclaimed radical reformulation of economic theory was a response to the failure of standard theory
to offer a coherent and consistent explanation of what was, at the time he
wrote, a virtually self-evident attribute of capitalism: the tendency to
generate stagnation and great depressions accompanied by financial collapse. His theory not only explained stagnation as well as boom, depression, and financial phenomena in an integrated fashion—making the
anomaly of orthodox theory, the usual of Keynesian Theory—but it also
led to a set of policy proposals to offset the consequences of depression
and financial collapse. In addition, even though Keynes preferred a re-
formed capitalism to the alternative of thoroughgoing socialism, his
analysis carried a serious critique of capitalism. In Keynes's own view
his theory implied that the existing order should be replaced by a much
more egalitarian economy, based upon a dominance of social control over
investment. As the private, profit-motivated decisions to invest cannot
guarantee a reasonable approximation to full employment; " a somewhat
comprehensive socialization of investment" (GT, p. 378) will prove
necessary.

A number of reasons may be advanced for the aborting of the
Keynesian Revolution. Like many other seminal and original works, The
General Theory is a very clumsy statement. Much of the old theory is still
there, and a great deal of the new is imprecisely stated and poorly

explained. Keynes stated in the preface that "The composition of this book has been for the author a long struggle of escape . . . from habitual modes of thought and expression" (*GT*, p. viii); however, his escape from the old was not complete. He acknowledged that the old ideas ramified "into every corner of our minds" (*GT*, p. viii). As a result, at a number of critical points, especially in some of the passages dealing with investment, interest rates, and the valuation of assets, he conceded much to the classical school. Thus in interpreting *The General Theory* to determine what is vital and what is not essential to the radical revision Keynes believed he was formulating, it is necessary both to prune away concessions made to the old—concessions which were either inadvertent, due to the hold of the old over Keynes's thought processes, or consciously opportunistic, due to Keynes's desire to speed the adoption of correct policy, if not of correct analysis—and to extend, complete, and draw further inferences from the innovative elements.

A further reason that the revolution was aborted may be that Keynes participated hardly at all in the interpretative debate that followed, a debate which has continued to this day. Most intellectual revolutions are made by the young. Marx, Darwin, Freud, and Einstein are examples of leaders of intellectual revolutions who had long careers after they put forth their new view. They participated fully in the transition from the clumsy original to the better, more elegant, and polished statement of the new theory. They were around to point out that an interpretation had not gotten something quite right, that a particular bit of evidence showed exactly what they meant, and that the new concepts had implications beyond those recognized in the initial statement.

Keynes lived for a decade after the appearance of *The General Theory*; but this was not a decade of tranquillity and scientific pursuit. In the first year after the appearance of *The General Theory* Keynes did undertake a few pieces of explanation, clarification, and rebuttal. The rebuttal to Viner's review,[11] an essay on interest rates in a volume honoring Irving Fisher,[12] and a reply to Ohlin in the *Economic Journal*[13] are three

---

[11]Keynes, "The General Theory of Employment," pp. 209–23. The only reviews he replied to were those in the *Quarterly Journal of Economics* of November 1936; his rebuttal was concentrated on Viner's lengthy review, which Keynes characterized as "the most important of the four comments," making only polite or caustic comments in passing on the reviews by Leontief, Tausig, and D. H. Robertson.

[12]Keynes, "The Theory of the Rate of Interest," pp. 418–24.

[13]Keynes, "Alternative Theories of the Rate of Interest," pp. 241–52.

important ventures in explanation and clarification which Keynes under-took after *The General Theory* appeared.

In the light of these post–*General Theory* bits by Keynes it is difficult to understand how the standard interpretation and formalization, which in the main tradition took off from J. R. Hicks's article, "Mr. Keynes and the 'Classics,' "[14] became the accepted interpretation of liquidity pref-erence as equivalent to a variable velocity in the quantity theory. Perhaps the explanation lies in the way in which Hicks formalized and simplified the model. Hicks gave the economics discipline a simple, neat exposition, using diagrams equivalent to those familiar from supply-and-demand analysis. Keynes in his rebuttal to Viner clearly and suc-cinctly set out, without the use of diagrams, or algebra, a model of asset valuation under conditions of uncertainty which was both strange to the profession and more difficult for his colleagues than Hicks's simple con-struct. In presenting the essential substance of *The General Theory*, great weight should be placed upon Keynes's post–*General Theory* pieces which were designed to clarify the logical structure, content, and implications of *The General Theory*.

Keynes's participation in the purely scientific aspects of the Keynesian Revolution ended with his heart attack in early 1937, soon after *The General Theory* appeared. Keynes really did not resume full activity until after World War II had gotten under way. The heart attack and the war meant that Keynes never fully participated in the hammering out of a polished version of Keynesian doctrine from the rough statement con-tained in *The General Theory*.

The coming of World War II meant that Keynes was soon to be ensconced as a gray eminence and gadfly in the government. In the government the theoretical analysis of expenditures and resource use developed in *The General Theory*, for situations where aggregate demand was a variable ratio to available output, was transformed into a tool for planning overall resource use in a war economy. A reformulation of Keynesian ideas for a regime of resource scarcity rather than one of inadequate aggregate demand was necessary if these ideas were to be applied in the context of a great war. The determination of adequate private investment and of how private investment decisions are related to monetary, financial, and expectational variables is not the issue in war-

[14]Hicks, "Mr. Keynes and the 'Classics,' " pp. 147–59.

time economics, when direct controls constrain private investment and the government assures the financing of permitted activities. One use of the Keynesian formulation in a war framework naturally focused on how consumption could be constrained so as to free resources for war purposes. Thus the emphasis upon the consumption function as a critical rather than a passive element in Keynesian theory was a natural outgrowth of the application of the theory to the economic problems that war presented.

Inasmuch as war, like socialism, focuses on the allocation of scarce resources, and as this is an economic situation in which neoclassical economics is at home, the initial wartime applications of Keynesian economics quite naturally focused on those aspects of the theory that had the most in common with classical economics. The quantitative mode of economic analysis in terms of flow (income) aggregates, which was successful in overall war planning, emerged in the postwar period as econometric forecasting. In spite of twenty-five years of postwar experimenting with econometric forecasting models, the theories of money, finance, and investment embedded in them are more relevant to an economy operating under constraints from real resources, with an absence of financial constraints and inducements, than to one where demand determines the utilization level for various resources and financial considerations vitally affect demand.

Wartime financing in both Britain and the United States resulted in a large increase in the holdings of government and bank liabilities by households, firms, and non-bank financial institutions. As a result the fragile financial system of the 1930s was replaced by a robust financial system in the first postwar decades. The economic problems cast up by the world in the first postwar decades were not of the type contemplated by Keynes in *The General Theory*. Money and finance did not operate as vital determinants of real aggregate demand in the decades immediately following World War II.

As the sixties progressed, eminent economists—especially those associated with government policy formulation—who in their own minds were disciples of Keynes, were announcing that endogenous business cycles and domestic financial crises were a thing of the past, now that the secrets of economic policy had been unlocked. The observations that were anomalies from the perspective of the standard theory before *The General Theory*—the anomalies that gave occasion for the intellectual crises within which *The General Theory* was born—were not replicated in the thirty years following the appearance of *The General Theory*. In the entire history of the United States from the days of Washington to the days of Franklin D. Roosevelt, no span of thirty years can be found without some serious depressions and disturbing financial traumas. The first meaningful financial disturbance in the United States after World War II occurred in the autumn of 1966, more than thirty-three years after Roosevelt's inauguration.

Economics and other sciences whose data are generated by history are not like the experimental natural sciences with respect to anomalous observations. In the natural sciences an experiment once made that leads to an observation difficult for standard theory to explain is henceforth always present. Any competent practitioner can replicate this observation. In economics if history over a thirty-year period does not cast up observations with at least a family resemblance to a financial panic or a deep depression, then arguments to the effect that these anomalies are myths, or that what happened can be explained by measurement errors, human (policy) errors, or transitory institutional flaws which have since been corrected, may be put forth and gain acceptance. That is, the view arises that the disturbing problem that established a need for a new theory 'never' really occurred. Thus an economic theory based upon a business cycle associated with a financial-instability view of how the economy operates can be replaced by theory with an equilibrium and steady-growth perspective, because the relevant observations to substantiate the cyclical, financial-instability view cannot be made. This is what took place as the forties, fifties, and sixties spun their tales of war and apparent economic success—a success achieved with the aid of apparently appropriate monetary and fiscal policy.

Another reason that the Keynesian Revolution was aborted, and that we do not now have an elegantly stated, thoroughgoing Keynesian theory, is that the older standard theory, after assimilating a few Keynesian phrases and relations, made what was taken to be real scientific advances. Even though economists had often argued as if the laissez-faire proposition, about the common good being served as if by an invisible hand by a regime of free competitive markets, were firmly established, it is only since World War II that mathematical economists have been able to achieve elegant formal proofs of the validity of this proposition for a market economy—albeit under such highly restrictive assumptions that the practical relevance of the theory is suspect. The presumed validation of the laissez-faire proposition was taken to mean that if monetary—or aggregate—theory could, so to say, ride piggy-back on mathematical general-equilibrium theory, then the behavior of a system with money could also have optimal properties.

It turns out that the accomplishments of pure theory during the 1950s and 1960s are more apparent than real, when the problems of a financially sophisticated capitalist economy are under consideration. As yet none of the significant theorems have been shown to carry over to a regime where time and thus uncertainty exists and in which money and finance are given meaningful definitions in terms of the need to finance positions in real wealth and investment.[15] Thus the purely intellectual pursuit of consistency between what was taken to be an elegant and scientifically valid microeconomics and a presumably crude macroeconomics has turned out to have been a false pursuit: microeconomics is at least as crude as macroeconomics. The success of each depends upon making meaningful abstractions, and neither can explain all of economic reality in a consistent manner.

Finally, the Keynesian Revolution may have been aborted because the standard neoclassical interpretation led to a policy posture that was adequate for the time. Given the close memory of the Great Depression in the immediate post–World War II era, all that economic policy really had to promise was that the Great Depression would not recur. The simple rules of fiscal policy, which took the form of government contracts and tax abatements to sustain the profitability of capital assets, succeeded in guiding policy so that a close approximation to full employment was in fact achieved and sustained. The standard interpretation leads to the conservative conclusion that only trivial changes in the institutions of capitalism are necessary to assure that crises do not occur and that depressions are mild. Questions as to whether the success of standard policy could be sustained and questions of "for whom" and "what kind" and about the nature of full employment were not raised. The Keynesian Revolution may have been aborted because the lessons drawn from the standard interpretation not only did not require any radical reformulation of the society but also were sufficient for the rather undemanding performance criteria that were ruling.

[15]Hahn, *On the Notion of Equilibrium in Economics.*

As the economy of the 1970s emerges it seems as if some of the economic phenomena of the 1920s and 1930s are being replayed. Financial instability and crises, now labeled crunches and squeezes, as well as periods of relative stagnation are occurring. Inflation now seems to be a chronic ailment of even the sophisticated economies. The world is now performing in ways that can be interpreted as anomalous from the point of view of the current standard theory. In these circumstances a radical reformulation of economic theory, such as Keynes attempted, once again seems attractive. The synthesis of classical formulations and Keynesian constructs that Professor Joan Robinson has characterized as Bastard Keynesianism seems to be dissolving. In the light of these developments, it seems worthwhile to extract from Keynes the ingredients that point to a radical reformulation of economic theory and to determine if these ingredients can serve as a point of departure for a new attempt at an alternative to the standard theory.

In what follows we will:

1.   Present an exposition of standard, or conventional Keynesian doctrine, ending with the neoclassical synthesis.

2.   Derive an alternative interpretation of Keynes—one which builds upon those aspects of *The General Theory* that emphasize investment in a world where business cycles exist and engender uncertainty. This leads to a quite different image of how the world operates than that embodied in current standard theory.

3.   Examine the policy and philosophical implications of the alternative interpretation of Keynes.

◄ 2 ►

The Conventional Wisdom: The Standard Interpretation of Keynes

INTRODUCTION

In order to make precise the way in which the promise of *The General Theory*, to radically change economic theory, has not been realized, we need to identify those concepts in *The General Theory* which are and those which are not a part of today's mainstream macroeconomics. We need to make clear how the neglected ideas of Keynes lead to views about both the economy's behavior and the possibilities and limitations of economic policy that are quite different from current conventional macroeconomics. This means that we will have to sharpen some of the clumsy presentations and fill in some gaps in the argument of *The General Theory*. This is necessary, for the neglected ideas have neither been made as precise nor been as fully worked out in academic debates as have the formulations which have been integrated into mainstream macroeconomics. However, before we turn to a presentation of an alternative interpretation of *The General Theory*, we need to survey the current standard interpretations of Keynes's work, so that what we deviate from is clear.

Three sets of macroeconomic models based on a selection of ideas from *The General Theory* have been hammered out on the forges of academic discussion. One set is based upon the consumption function to the exclusion of well-nigh all the remainder of *The General Theory*. A second set consists of models which formalize the requirement for the simultaneous satisfaction of commodity and money-market equilibrium conditions. In turn, the second set is transformed into a third set of models which use production-function and naïve preference-system ideas to derive the equilibrium conditions in the labor market, along with the commodity and money-market equilibrium conditions of the second set of models.

In the third set of models an inconsistency among the equilibrium conditions in the various sets of markets can arise. In principle these inconsistencies can be resolved in a number of ways. In the particular resolution that has dominated the literature, money and financial assets are introduced into the consumption function. This leads to a "neoclassical" model in which the labor-market equilibrium dominates in the theoretical determination of system equilibrium. Such a final modification of the conventional Keynesian system—in which labor-market equilibrium sets the stage for other markets—not only thoroughly violates the spirit of *The General Theory* but it also returns the argument to the world of the "classical economy."

The introduction of money and financial variables as endogenously determined parameters, which shift or position the relations in a model based upon ingredients and constructs introduced by Keynes, is the key element in the formulation of the neoclassical synthesis. Until the introduction of such financial reactions, the various models based upon concepts derived from *The General Theory* indicated that an unplanned capitalist economy was flawed, in that its endogenous processes did not necessarily lead to a full-employment equilibrium. The introduction of these financial variables in the consumption function led to a model without such an in-principle flaw, even though many hold that the financial-variable mechanism is too slow and too weak to be relied upon for practical policy. In the light of these models, if nevertheless capitalism, in its demand and employment attributes, remains flawed, the explanation must lie elsewhere than in the relations considered within these models. This becomes the ground for the views that the evident flaw in capitalism with respect to the achievement and maintenance of full employment is due either to rigidities such as rigid wages that prevent market processes from operating, or to nonessential institutional flaws—such as imperfections in the banking system, or the failure of management of monetary systems—which shock the system out of equilibrium and offset the operations of the equilibrating process. It follows also that either appropriate management of economic policy or rather minor institutional changes can overcome the rigidities and prevent the shocks, thus eliminating the flaws. These models become the rationale for an activist, managed approach to economic policy in a capitalist economy and for the view that fundamental reforms are not necessary.

The first set of models we will discuss, the consumption-function models, ignore monetary phenomena. They do not lead to models which can fully explore the impact of government debt-financing of a portion of its spending. On the other hand, balanced-budget and fiscal-drag theorems can be derived from these models. Furthermore, the consumption function is easily mated with accelerator or capital-coefficient formulations of investment behavior. Mechanical accelerator-multiplier business cycle models as well as capital-coefficient growth models result from such unions. In addition to its role in the building of such dynamic models, the consumption function provides the intellectual basis for most of the large-scale structural econometric models that have been developed for forecasting purposes. Much of the popular policy discussion that is called Keynesian is dominated by models that are based on the consumption function, to the virtual exclusion of the more sophisticated models which allow for monetary and investment interactions.

Keynes was almost exclusively a monetary economist. The second set of models whose lineage may be traced to *The General Theory* consists of various models in which investment and portfolio relations are added to the consumption (saving) function. The standard formulation is an outgrowth of a model that was developed by J. R. Hicks[1] in an effort to explicate the links he saw between *The General Theory* and the so-called classics: the ideas and theories embodied in the work of Marshall, his predecessors, and his followers. The model developed by Hicks introduces explicitly the demand and supply of money into the income determination setup. This framework (usually called the *IS-LM* framework) was the basis of Professor Alvin Hansen's work detailing policy

---

[1]Hicks, "Mr. Keynes and The 'Classics,' " pp. 147–59.

prescriptions for the United States in the period just before and immediately after World War II; as a result this approach is often called the
Hicks-Hansen model.[2]

The addition of an aggregate labor market to the commodity and
money markets of the Hicks-Hansen framework enables us to make the
classical model, in which the labor market dominates, explicit. This
model also enables us to show that a dynamic less-than-full-employment
equilibrium is possible, for the impact of excess supply in the labor
market may be inefficient in increasing aggregate demand. A further
modification of the Hicks-Hansen framework introduces wealth and
monetary variables into the consumption relation. This modification,
mainly associated with the work of Patinkin,[3] leads to a model in which
the proposition that money is neutral, in the sense that the equilibrium
values of all economic variables except the price level are independent of
the money supply, is conditionally valid. The significant necessary conditions for this to hold are that the money supply be of an outside
nature—such as government debt or specie—and that if excess supply in
the labor market exists it lead to a reduction in money wages and prices.

Once the neutrality of money is shown to be valid in principle, macroeconomic theory has come full circle, for this is the key theorem of the
classical quantity theory. In his review of *The General Theory* W. W.
Leontief argued that a fundamental assumption of general equilibrium
theory is that "all supply and demand functions, with prices taken as
independent variables and quantity as a dependent one, are homogeneous functions of the zero degree."[4] In a short rebuttal Keynes explicitly
denies the validity of this homogeneity postulate, on the grounds that
"there was abundant evidence from experience to contradict this postulate; and that, in any case, it is for those who make a highly special
assumption to justify it, rather than for those who dispense with it, to
prove a general negative." Furthermore, Keynes argues that the postulate
that demand functions are homogeneous of degree zero "enters into the
orthodox theoretical scheme . . . in connection with the part played by
the quantity of money in determining the rate of interest."[5] That is, in

[2] See Hansen, *Monetary Theory and Fiscal Policy.*

[3] Patinkin, *Money, Interest, and Prices, An Integration of Monetary and Value Theory.*

[4] Leontief, "The Fundamental Assumption of Mr. Keynes' Monetary Theory of Unemployment," p. 193.

[5] Keynes, "The General Theory of Employment," p. 209; henceforth cited as *QJE* in the
text.

Keynes's scheme the rate of interest is *not* homogeneous of degree zero with respect to the quantity of money; in the orthodox scheme of things this heroic assumption is crucial to the argument.

Thus the quantity theory of money, which Keynes endeavored to set to rest, has apparently swept the field, at least on the plane of academic economic theory, by assimilating what are taken to be Keynes's special insights. For a short time in the late 1960s and early 1970s a naïve version of the quantity theory, in the guise of the doctrines of monetarism, had a revival as a guide to economic policy.

In this chapter we will put forth the various orthodox Keynesian models as well as the core neoclassical model. In the following chapters we will draw from *The General Theory*, and the post–*General Theory* explications by Keynes, the views which have been ignored in the development of the main-line tradition. These ignored portions combined with some of the ingredients used in the standard models lead to an alternative and radically different interpretation of *The General Theory*.

CONSUMPTION FUNCTION MODELS

In *The General Theory* the consumption-function construct serves the purpose of identifying the passive, or determined, component of aggregate demand: in no sense is the consumption function "the heart of modern macroeconomics,"[6] if modern macroeconomics is identified with Keynes. In Keynes's view it is, if an anatomical analogy is necessary, the passive skeleton of macroeconomics which nevertheless conditions the system's responses to stimuli.

The passive nature of consumption expenditures has two aspects. For the working classes, who have no financial resources, the prior, simultaneous, or assured receipt of income from wages, or transfer payments, is necessary if consumption spending is to take place. For the property-owning classes, with financial resources, the ideology of maintaining capital intact tends to make consumption spending depend upon net rather than gross income. Thus as it is assumed initially that consumption expenditures do not depend upon external financing to any significant extent, they do not leave a financial residue in the form of contracts which entail payment commitments.

The validity of this view of consumption is attenuated as institutions

---

[6] Ackley, *Macroeconomic Theory*, p. viii.

and usages change. Thus whether and the extent to which financial considerations affect consumption change in time. The growth of consumer-financing arrangements—first in the 1920s and again since World War II—has weakened the connection between worker's income and household spending. The growth of welfare schemes and transfer payments has also attenuated the connection between employment and consumer spending. Furthermore, given the facts about income distribution in a capitalist economy such as the United States, a very substantial part (a low estimate might be 20 percent) of total consumption expenditures is made by the upper 5 percent of the population in income distribution. These 5 percent of the population have financial resources and are affected by the value the equity market places upon the stock of capital assets. Thus the dependence of consumption spending upon near-term income from employment—which was and remains a fine first approximation for use in theory construction—is a less valid empirical assumption for the United States in the 1970s than it was for Britain, and the United States, thirty-five years earlier.

A major theme in economic theory is that economic growth requires accumulation and that the relative prosperity of different lands depends upon the results of past accumulations which are available for use in production. Accumulation in turn depends upon the existence of a surplus, i.e., of a positive difference between output and the sum of current-period consumption and capital consumption. In Marx it was the inability of workers to purchase back what they produced that led to the surplus. In Keynes the fundamental psychological law guiding consumption determines how the surplus behaves as other variables—especially income—change. Although class ideas with respect to consumption are alluded to in *The General Theory*, and although class income affects the saving propensities in the work of Keynesian economists, such as N. Kaldor and J. Robinson, in general in the mainstream Keynesian literature the law for the determination of the surplus (i.e., the consumption function) treats income as a homogeneous glob in determining consumption behavior.

The contention that "the consumption function is the heart of macroeconomics" has a degree of plausibility insofar as econometric research has had some success in estimating empirical consumption functions. These estimated consumption functions serve in turn as the basis for models looking toward economic forecasting and even control. Estimated consumption functions are at the center of a generation of econometric models oriented toward policy. However, this very amenability to econometric analysis is evidence that consumption behaves as the predictable passive-reactor part of total endogenous spending. The laws guiding the passive reactor, being simpler, are easier to uncover than the laws guiding the active driving forces in income determination.

The idea that consumption is a determined function of income, basically independent of monetary and financial influences, leads to a simple model that has become the "first" exercise in income-determination theory in most textbooks. However, because consumption in turn can be divided into various types of durables, nondurables, automobiles, services, housing, etc., the simple model can be made as "complex" as an analyst desires without any significant increase in conceptual sophistication. As a part of the large-scale models of the 1950s and 1960s, the consumption-function model, sectored for different types of consumption, became one of the major pieces of econometric gadgetry.

The simplistic consumption-function model finds little support in Keynes. His discussion of the consumption function is rather short; Book Three, "The Propensity to Consume," is but 43 pages, whereas Book Four, "The Inducement to Invest," runs for 114 pages. Keynes viewed the "employment directly employed in investment as the primary employment" (*GT*, p. 113); the employment in consumption was secondary, or derived.

Keynes's statement of the rationale for the consumption function is:

> The fundamental psychological law, upon which we are entitled to depend with great confidence both *a priori* and from our detailed knowledge of human nature and from the detailed facts of experience, is that men are disposed, as a rule and on the average to increase their consumption as their income increases, but not by as much as the increase in their income. [*GT*, p. 96]

The actual precise numbers vary with the time span under analysis as well as with other more narrowly economic variables. It is of special validity "where we have short periods in view, as in the case of the so-called cyclical fluctuations of employment during which habits . . . are not given time enough to adapt themselves to changed objective circumstance" (*GT*, p. 97). "Thus a rising income will often be accompanied by increasing saving, and a falling income by decreasing saving, on a greater scale at first than subsequently" (*GT*, p. 97).

The cyclical consumption-income relation embodies an initial stability of absolute consumption standards, which is followed by an adjustment toward a longer-run sustained ratio of consumption to income: the consumption-income ratio adjusts upward as increased income is sustained and adjusts downward as decreased income is prolonged. This lagging relation between consumption changes and income changes in a cyclical environment has been interpreted by later analysts as indicating that consumption is more closely related to a concept, often labeled permanent income, that when measured averages past incomes, than to current (or recent), measured (or actual) income.

In the academic discussion since the appearance of *The General Theory* the concept of consumption and the ideas as to the determinants of consumption have undergone considerable change. To Keynes consumption, for the purpose of employment theory, was a part of aggregate effective demand. Aggregate effective demand, when introduced into the inverse of the aggregate-supply function, generated the demand for labor. Thus consumption to Keynes always involved current production.

In the "truth" which the preference system of neoclassical economic theory hypothesizes, we "consume" the services that flow from durable consumer goods—such as automobiles—as well as the services that flow from the stock of houses. Thus this theory calls for a concept of consumption which adds to the currently consumed part of current output the flow of services from past accumulations of consumer durables and housing. This concept treats almost all the production of current consumer durables and housing as if they were a form of investment. This flow-of-services concept of consumption is more satisfactory from the point of view of neoclassical economic theory, in that it is consistent with the view of consumption that is used in microeconomic theory. However, it is misleading from the perspective of employment theory. From that perspective, what is needed is a theory of household spending on "output" that during the current period uses labor, regardless of when this output will be used and how the spending is financed.

The appropriate income concept to use in the consumption function has been a subject of debate in the literature. One view looks to permanent or life-cycle rather than current income as the determinant of consumption spending. These concepts of income are consistent with views that a household plans its consumption over a longer or even a lifetime period. Basically a unit's permanent or lifetime income depends upon the returns the factors it owns will earn as inputs into the economy's production processes. Because the "marginal productivity" of a factor input in a full-employment world does not change all that rapidly, a household has a good idea of the real income that its owned factors will earn. Thus it is assumed that the household has, and those it has financial dealings with have, a good idea of its expected real income; and real consumption is adjusted to expected real income.

Once some of the consumption expenditures are externally financed, and units accept a cyclical and uncertain (rather than an equilibrium and certain) view of income over time, then the standard permanent or life-cycle income concept becomes less relevant for determining current-period consumption expenditures. In its place a modified permanent-income concept which allows for the impact of uncertainty and house-hold financial conditions upon current spending becomes relevant. Whereas the standard permanent-income concept tends to make consumption behave in a stabilizing manner during cyclical fluctuations, this alternative view contains the possibility that consumption will behave in a procyclical manner.

In addition, apart from short-period changes in the level of income, it was obvious to Keynes that a higher absolute level of income will tend, as a rule, to widen the absolute gap between income and consumption. "These reasons will lead as a rule, to a greater proportion of income being saved as real income increases. But whether or not a greater proportion is saved . . . when its [a modern community's] real income is increased, it will not increase its consumption by an equal absolute amount" (*GT*, p. 97).

Especially as consumption is the passive and determined rather than the active and determining factor, its precise behavior in response to objective economic factors is of great importance. When the behavior of consumption is understood, the quantitative measures of the effect of changes in the determining factors, investment and government expenditures, will be known.

Keynes listed a number of objective factors other than changes in income that affect the propensity to consume. Of special significance for later work was the precise definition of income for the varying income-receiving classes: how net—or what later might be called disposable—income differed from gross income and how gains and losses in capital values which do not enter into measured income affect consumption. In addition, Keynes discussed the effect of interest rates, anticipated price-level changes, fiscal and financial policy of business and government, and expectations of future income upon consumption. After summarizing these influences Keynes concluded that "the propensity to consume may be considered a fairly stable function. . . . Windfall changes in capital values will be capable of changing this propensity to consume, and substantial changes in the rate of interest and fiscal policy may make some difference" (*GT*, pp. 95–96). Nevertheless, "the aggregate income measured in terms of the wage-unit is, as a rule, the principal variable upon which the consumption-constituent of the aggregate demand function will depend" (*GT*, p. 96).

The consumption function, in Keynes's view, was of importance because it led directly to the multiplier which explained how "the changes in the amount of employment will be a function of the net changes in the amount of investment" (*GT*, p. 114). It was "to the general principle of the multiplier to which we have to look for an explanation of how fluctuation in the amount of investment, which are a comparatively small proportion of the national income, are capable of generating fluctuations in aggregate employment and income so much greater in amplitude than themselves" (*GT*, p. 122). Thus the long-run, or secular, consumption-income relation fades into the background. To Keynes the cyclical consumption function is of major significance, for the major problem he set is to explain cyclical fluctuations.

In simple linear form the consumption function model is written as

$$Y = C + I$$
$$C = a_0 + a_1 Y \qquad a_0 > 0, \quad 0 < a_1 < 1$$
$$I = I_0$$

where a_1 is the marginal propensity to consume, Y is income, C is consumption and I is investment. Because in this model there is no way in which price-level changes can affect system behavior, price-level changes can be ignored; it really does not matter if Y, C, and I are taken to be real or nominal.

This gives rise to the multiplier relation

$$Y = \frac{a_0 + I}{1 - a_1} \quad \text{where} \quad \frac{1}{1 - a_1} = k, \quad \text{the multiplier so that}$$

$$Y = k a_0 + k I.$$

This model can be readily expanded: for example, consumption can be a function of disposable income, Y_D, which is income, Y, minus taxes, T, and aggregate demand can be written as including government spending, G:

$$Y = C + I + G$$
$$Y_D = Y - T$$
$$C = a_0 + a_1 Y_D \quad \text{or}$$
$$C = a_0 + a_1 (Y - T).$$

The multiplier relations for this model become

$$Y = \frac{a_0 + I + G - a_1 T}{1 - a_1}$$

where $1/(1 - a_1)$ is the multiplier for investment and government spending, and $a_1/(1 - a_1)$ is the multiplier for taxes. If

$$\Delta Y = \frac{\Delta G}{1 - a_1} - \frac{a_1}{1 - a_1} \Delta T, \quad \text{and} \quad \Delta G = \Delta T,$$

$$\text{then} \quad \Delta Y = \Delta G,$$

which is the simplest balanced-budget theorem; that is, an equal increase in government expenditures and tax receipts lead to an equal increase in income.

If we further postulate that income taxes are important, so that taxes become a function of income,

$$T = \gamma_0 + \gamma_1 Y,$$

where γ_0 and γ_1 are politically determined parameters of the tax schedule, we then have that

$$Y = C + I + G$$
$$Y_D = Y - \gamma_0 - \gamma_1 Y$$
$$C = a_0 + a_1(Y - \gamma_0 - \gamma_1 Y).$$

In this model the multiplier relations become

$$Y = \frac{a_0 - a_1 \gamma_0 + I + G}{1 - a_1 + \gamma_1 a_1}.$$

As $1 - a_1 + \gamma_1 a_1 > 1 - a_1$, the multiplier for a model which allows taxes to be a function of income is smaller than for a model in which taxes are independent of income. Thus an income-related tax scheme acts as a drag upon the expansionary effect of an increase in investment or government spending and offsets some of the contractionary effect of a decline in investment or government spending.

The function $C_t = a_0 + a_1 Y$ may be joined to a formulation of investment based upon a production relation $Y = vk$. In this relation $\Delta Y = v\Delta K$, or $I = (1/v) \Delta Y = \beta \Delta Y$, where v is the output per unit of capital coefficient and β is the capital per unit of output. The linkage might take the form $I_t = \beta(Y_{t-1} - Y_{t-2})$ where $(Y_{t-1} - Y_{t-2})$ is the latest change in income whose size is known at time t. For symmetry, let us write $C_t = \alpha Y_{t-1}$, so that consumption depends upon the latest income that is known to have been earned. Combining the two we get

$$Y_t = (\alpha + \beta)Y_{t-1} - \beta Y_{t-2}$$

which is one form of the accelerator-multiplier model.

As is illustrated in diagram 2.1, this second-order difference equation can yield a number of different types of time series of income depending upon the values of α and β. If $\beta > 1$ the time series will be explosive; if $\beta < 1$ the time series will be dampened. If $(\alpha + \beta)^2 - 4\beta < 0$, then the time series is cyclical; if the inequality is reversed it is monotonic. Thus the accelerator-multiplier formulation is capable of generating a variety of time series—it can be used as the basis for mechanical expositions of ideas about cyclical experience. In the next chapters it will be argued that such a mechanical explanation of the business cycle is inconsistent with the major thrust of Keynes's views.

The consumption function also can be used to generate mechanical models of the growth process. Assume that in order to produce one unit of output v units of capital are needed. Assume that s percent of income is saved at full employment. We then have that

$$I = sY, \quad \text{and} \quad Y = vK \quad \text{so that} \quad \Delta Y = vI.$$

This gives us

$$\frac{\Delta Y}{v} = sY \quad \text{or} \quad \frac{\Delta Y}{Y} = sv.$$

If we call $\Delta Y/Y$ the rate of growth, g, we have that

$$g = sv.$$

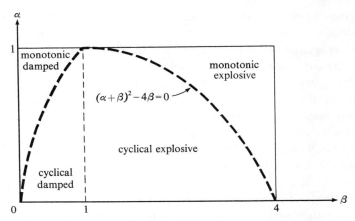

Diagram 2.1   TIME   SERIES   GENERATED   BY   ACCELERATOR-
           MULTIPLIER MODELS

Thus the consumption function, in its simplest form, can be used as the basis for two apparently dynamic sets of models: accelerator-multiplier models and one-sector-growth models.

The simple consumption-function model may be broken down into types of consumption. For example, $C_1 \ldots C_n$ may be various types of consumption, such as services, nondurables, and durables, and $I_1 \ldots I_n$ may be various types of investment, such as housing, utilities, manufacturing, and inventories. Some of the particular types of consumption and investment may be functions of income of past periods, stocks of such items outstanding, as well as interest rates. No matter how complicated the subdivisions of consumption and investment may be the model remains of the form

$$Y = \Sigma k_i X_i$$

where k_i is the appropriate multiplier and X_i the related exogenous or predetermined variables.

The obvious step that should be taken if such ideas are to be applied is to estimate empirically the various consumption, investment, and other functions that enter into the model so that the various k's may be derived. The truths about the world that these models are capable of developing are limited by their postulates. The empirical estimation of short-period changes in investment has not been one of the outstanding successes of econometric work. Many of the models that are used have given up on estimating investment from functional relations presumed to capture economic regularities; instead, they rely upon survey data—questionnaires to businessmen—for their estimates of I.

In their various forms, early econometric forecasting models did not find a large or significant role for interest rates, monetary phenomena, or financial interrelations in determining income. As a representation of the economy these models tended to indicate that the power of fiscal policy was unrelated to the financial circumstances within which fiscal policy operated. These models built upon one facet of *The General Theory*. They were in their gross simplicity a misrepresentation of Keynes's views. The failure, or success, of the financially naïve econometric forecasting models does not constitute a test of the validity of Keynes's theory.

Fundamental to Keynes's ideas in *The General Theory* is the notion of uncertainty as a major determining element in portfolio choice and thus in investment. Fundamental to the fiscal policy variants of econometric models based upon the consumption function is the notion that, if policy instruments are set at a particular level, the economy can be fine-tuned so that full employment is maintained in perpetuity. Keynes's view leads to the idea that if full employment is maintained for a while, beliefs as to the "uncertainties" faced by entrepreneurs and wealth owners will change. As a result, full employment once sustained implies an explosive increase in demand. To Keynes the uncertainty effects and financial repercussions of any state undermined its stability. Such Keynesian notions are foreign to the simple consumption-function models and their naïve, though complicated, econometric forecasting offshoots.

THE IS-LM FRAMEWORK

Professor Hicks introduced the most widely used expository-analytical apparatus in contemporary macroeconomics, the *IS-LM* diagram, in an article whose aim was quite explicitly the reconciliation of "Mr. Keynes and the 'Classics.' "[7] This framework served as the skeleton for much of the argumentation by Professor A. Hansen, who was most important in hammering out the American version of standard Keynesianism. Thus the *IS-LM* approach is often called the Hicks-Hansen framework. The thrust of Hicks's argument is that in *The General Theory* Keynes qualified but did not repudiate the sophisticated versions

[7]Hicks, "Mr. Keynes and The 'Classics,' " pp. 147–59.

of classical theory. As we will note later, this Hicksian position is very similar in its thrust to the interpretation of *The General Theory* offered by Professor Viner in his review, the only review of *The General Theory* that drew forth an extended comment from Keynes. Keynes explicitly repudiated Viner's interpretation of the structure of the argument in *The General Theory*.

In Hicks's article the various representations of the ideas in *The General Theory* are introduced without citation or documentation. It is noted "that the entertainment value . . . [of *The General Theory*] is considerably enhanced by its satiric aspect."[8] Stock-flow relations, uncertainty, the emphasis on the essentially cyclical nature of investment, and the repeated references to the world as it is (the relevance of institutional detail) are important aspects of *The General Theory* that are ignored in Hicks's presentation. After noting that when the classical theory "is applied to the analysis of industrial fluctuations it gets into difficulties,"[9] Hicks treats *The General Theory* as being concerned primarily with the minor adjustments to the classical theory that are needed for this, presumably rather unimportant, application of theory.

Two points are worth noting before the Hicksian formalization is presented. The first is that the liquidity-preference function is treated by Hicks as a modification of the Marshallian demand-for-money function, with the addition of a proviso that the demand for cash be a function of the rate of interest as well as of transactions. After noting that Keynes has both income and the rate of interest in his demand for money, Hicks remarks that "With this revision, Mr. Keynes takes a big step to Marshallian orthodoxy and his theory becomes hard to distinguish from the revised and qualified Marshallian theories."[10]

The second is that the demand for investment is introduced in a most casual way. In introducing the "classical" model Hicks wrote: "In order to determine I_x (investment), we need two equations. One tells us that the amount of investment (looked at as a demand for capital) depends upon the rate of interest:

$$I_x = C(i).$$

This is what becomes the marginal-efficiency-of-capital schedule in Mr.

[8]Ibid., p. 147.
[9]Ibid., p. 150.
[10]Ibid., p. 153.

Keynes' work."[11] (The second required equation is the saving function.) The investment-demand function is identical in Hicks's versions of the classical and the Keynesian models; he changes the money demand and the saving-consumption functions of his classical model to generate a Keynesian model.

In terms of a phrasing which later became popular, Hicks works with a simultaneous system in which two markets are treated explicitly; the market for "money" and the market for "commodities." Equilibrium requires the simultaneous satisfaction of the ruling relations in each market.

In the Hicks-Hansen version of Keynes's theory, the market for money is encapsulated in an "endogenous" demand relation, which states that the demand for money, M_d is a function, L( ), of income, Y, and the interest rate, i, $M_d = L(i,Y)$ (what the interest rate is on is not specified in the Hicks article), and that the supply of money is exogenously determined by the "authorities"—presumably through open-market operations. For a given quantity of money in existence, $\overline{M}_s$, the demand function traces out loci of interest rates and real incomes that satisfy the demand for money constraint. This function (called the LM function) is in general upward sloping, although a (virtually) horizontal part for low incomes and a (virtually) vertical part for some high incomes are considered likely specifications (see diagram 2.2).

The commodity market consists of two parts. The first is a demand for investment given by the previously identified function:

$$I = I(i) \text{ (using today's conventional symbols)}$$

This is a negatively sloped function of the rate of interest. The second part is the consumption function, which is better treated as a saving function (saving = income − consumption). Given that $S = S(Y)$ and that $I = S$, we get $I(i) - S(Y) = 0$, which traces out a negatively sloped curve of (i, Y) points (called IS function). The intersection of IS and LM, defined for a given quantity of money, yields the interest rate and the level of "money income."

Hicks assumes explicitly that "w, the rate of money wages per head can be taken as given"; he assumes implicitly that the price level, $P = \lambda w$, so that money income and real income are related in a very

[11]Ibid., p. 149.

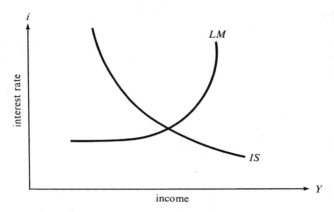

Diagram 2.2   *THE IS-LM DIAGRAM*

simple way. The implications for employment of various income levels are not explicitly discussed; there is no explicit treatment of labor-market conditions. The argument in this influential article is strangely truncated; it really says very little. However, given that wages and prices are fixed, "money" aggregate demand, or income, Y, can be transformed into a demand for labor. Thus employment is determined.

The *IS-LM* framework adds three relations to the simple consumption-function model: an investment-demand equation, a money-interest rate relation, and an exogenously determined money supply. Of fundamental importance in determining the validity of this framework as an interpretation of Keynes is the assumption that is made about money —both how the money supply is determined and how it enters into the determination of income and the interest rate.

It is quite clear that in *The General Theory* Keynes was concerned with three main types of assets. In chapter 12, "The State of Long Term Expectations," the valuation of the stock of capital assets is considered. Capital assets will generate prospective yields–cash flows, in the current terminology. The problem of the valuation of capital assets is attacked by assuming that "changes in the values of investments [meaning capital assets in Keynes's context] were solely due to changes in the expectation of their prospective yields and not at all to changes in the rate of interest at which these prospective yields are capitalized" (*GT*, p. 149).

The rate of interest, on the other hand, "is, in itself, nothing more than the inverse proportion between a sum of money and what can be obtained by parting with control over the money in exchange for a debt for a stated period of time" (*GT*, p. 167). However, "we can draw the line between "money" and "debts" at whatever point is most convenient for handling a particular problem" (*GT*, p. 167, footnote 1).

Thus Keynes envisions a two-step process: money and debts determine the rate of interest, which "In general discussion . . . [is] the complex of the various rates of interest current for different periods of time, i.e. for debts of different maturities" (*GT*, p. 167); and this rate of interest, combined with the prospective yield on capital assets, determines the value of capital assets. Keynes is not explicit as to who is the debtor on the contracts which determine the rate of interest—whether the debts be treasury bills, debts of merchants financing trade, or even debts of entrepreneurs financing positions in real capital.

For our purposes at this time, we need only insist that Keynes considered three types of assets: money which "As a rule" is assumed to be "co-extensive with bank deposits" (*GT*, p. 167); debts of an unspecified character which are contracts exchanging present money for future money; and real capital assets which are characterized by expected yields (cash flows) that may vary for a number of reasons, so that a rational man will not be certain about the cash flows that capital assets will generate.

The determination of investment, therefore, is a four-stage process in *The General Theory*. Money and debts determine an "interest rate"; long-term expectations determine the yield—or expected cash flows—from capital assets and current investment (i.e., the capital stock); the yield and the interest rate enter into the determination of the price of capital assets; and investment is carried to the point where the supply price of investment output equals the capitalized value of the yield. The simple *IS-LM* framework violates the complexity of the investment-determining process as envisaged by Keynes. In the literature, the puzzles with respect to the determination of investment put forth by Keynes have been ignored rather than solved.

For the present, we will accept the *IS-LM* formulation as a basis for our exposition of standard macroeconomics, with the proviso that in subsequent chapters we return to an examination of the foundations of investment theory. We have still to take up how the *IS-LM* approach is integrated into the neoclassical framework.

The *IS-LM* framework is more sophisticated than the simplistic consumption-function model in that it allows for the influence of money and permits the elasticities (shapes and positions) of the various functions to affect income. In particular, the view that the liquidity-preference function is a demand-for-money relation permits the introduction of the idea that in appropriate circumstances the demand for money may be infinitely elastic with respect to variations in the interest rate; that is, $M_D = L(i,Y)$ is such that for some range of incomes changing the money supply will not affect the interest rate. This liquidity trap presumably dominates in the immediate aftermath of a great depression or a financial crisis.

In the literature that developed around the *IS-LM* apparatus, three regions for monetary influence were defined in the *(Y,i)* plane (see diagram 2.3). In the liquidity trap region *(LT)* an increase in the money supply does not affect income and the interest rate; in the *Q* region an increase in the money supply is fully reflected in the level of money income; and in the intermediate region (labeled LM) both income and interest rates are affected by changes in the quantity of money. Thus in the *IS-LM* framework the results of a change in the quantity of money are not unambiguously "neutral": the interest rate might be affected. What actually happens after a change in the quantity of money is conditional upon the shape of the liquidity-preference function.

The rationale for the interest elasticity of the demand for money is

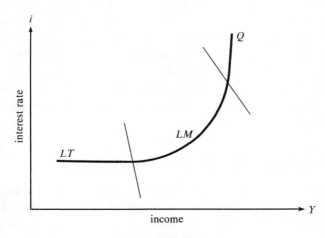

Diagram 2.3   THE LM DIAGRAM

broken into two parts: one is that the transactions demand is responsive to interest-rate variations; the other is that the portfolio, or asset, demand affects (determines) the interest rate on other assets.

At this juncture, the Hicksian model's vagueness as to what interest rate is under consideration becomes a particular point of weakness. The usual argument for the liquidity-trap portion of the schedule centers around the potential for capital loss that exists with a rise in interest rates: this implies that the interest rate in the liquidity-preference function is the long-term rate. On the other hand, the substitute for idle cash is a short-term asset, which argues that the interest rate in the liquidity-preference function is a short-term rate. One way around this difficulty is to assume that the pattern among interest rates is a constant—except that simple observation rules this view out. The difficulties raised by the question of the content of the Hicksian liquidity-preference function will be resolved as we reinterpret the liquidity-preference function as a schedule determining the demand price for assets.

In addition to the liquidity trap, the possibility exists that the *IS* curve may be inelastic with regard to interest—that a fall in the interest rate may not increase investment appreciably. Thus in the *IS-LM* formulation two slips between the monetary cup and the income lip are identified: an increase in the quantity of money may not lower the rate of interest, and if it lowers the rate of interest, this may not affect the amount of investment.

The Hicks-Hansen model, by making explicit the interdependence of the commodity and money markets in Keynes's thought, is a more accurate representation of his views than the simple consumption-function models. Nevertheless, because it did not explicitly consider the significance of uncertainty in both portfolio decisions and investment behavior, and because it was an equilibrium rather than a process interpretation of the model, it was an unfair and naïve representation of Keynes's subtle and sophisticated views.

THE LABOR MARKET AND THE IS-LM FRAMEWORK

A further step in the evolution of standard macroeconomics is the addition to the Hicks-Hansen framework of an explicit consideration of labor-market conditions. The models that result from the simultaneous consideration of labor, commodity, and money markets range in scope from models that exhibit properties which Keynes emphasized to models that are quite simply classical in nature. One outgrowth of the integration of the *IS-LM* framework with the labor market is the neo-classical synthesis, the model of the economy that is the core of standard macroeconomics.

With the statement in the next section of the neoclassical synthesis, we will have gone all the way down the wrong turn, for the main theorem of the neoclassical synthesis—that equilibrium at full employment is attainable by market processes—denies the theoretical or "general" validity of Keynes's view. This is so even though the neoclassical synthesis allows for the generation, and persistence, of unemployment due to rigidities and is consistent with the advocacy of "Keynesian" policy if the rigidities turn out to be dominant.

Once we have arrived at the neoclassical synthesis we will be in a position to examine, in the following chapters, in what way this result is due to a "wrong turn." Then we can set to work to construct a model that is truer to the spirit of *The General Theory*.

The labor market is usually introduced in aggregate analysis by generalizing the way in which specific labor markets are dealt with in conventional price theory. In order to do this, an aggregate-production function of the form

$$O = \Theta(K,N)$$

(where O = output, K = capital stock, and N = labor), such that

$$\frac{d\Theta}{dN} > 0 \quad \text{and} \quad \frac{d^2\Theta}{dN^2} < 0$$

is introduced (the marginal product of labor, $d\Theta/dN$, is positive for all N and decreasing as N increases). The aggregate-production function is used to determine both the demand function for labor and the output (real income) associated with each level of employment. The demand function for labor is the schedule of the marginal productivity of labor, with capital, the cooperating factor, fixed. The marginal productivity of labor decreases as employment increases; the schedule has a negative slope.

In *The General Theory* Keynes was mainly concerned with determining employment. However, he was very careful not to use an aggregate-production function in deriving the demand for labor. He first defined an aggregate-supply function, $Z = \phi(N)$, where Z is "the aggregate supply price of the output from employing N men" *(GT,* p. 25), and the inverse of the aggregate-supply function is $N = \phi^{-1}(Z)$. Inasmuch as aggregate demand, D, which is the sum of investment, consumption, and government demand, equals aggregate supply, the employment function can be written as depending upon aggregate demand:

$$N = \phi^{-1}(D).$$

By using arguments to the effect that the composition of each level of aggregate demand is quite well defined as between different types of output, Keynes concluded that the aggregation of particular employment functions to form a total employment function was legitimate.

The *IS-LM* framework generates the level of aggregate demand in real terms. Entering this aggregate demand into the employment function gives the level of employment. For simplicity, the supply of labor relation can be assumed to be infinitely elastic at an exogenously determined money wage.

Although Keynes did not use production-function ideas to determine the level of employment, he did use them to determine the price level associated with each money-wage rate and to determine how the price level varied for a given wage rate as employment varied. He assumed that the aggregate-supply function either increased linearly with employment or after employment reached a particular level it increased more rapidly than employment owing to a decreasing efficiency of labor in producing outputs. Inasmuch as the marginal sales proceeds due to hiring additional labor must equal or exceed the wage rate, Keynes reached the conclusion that the price level was proportional to the wage rate divided by the efficiency of labor—which can be identified as a marginal-productivity notion. Therefore, in the symbols of the marginal-productivity formulation, Keynes held that

$$P = \frac{W_0}{(d\Theta/dN)\,(N_E)} ,$$

that is, with a given money wage W_0, the price level P is inversely related to the incremental output due to labor at the ruling employment level, N_E. If $d\Theta/dN$ decreases when N_E increases, the price level for any given money wage increases when employment increases.

In the Keynesian formulation, labor market behavior which determines the course of W_0 is the proximate determinant of the price level. If this result does not contradict the standard view of the quantity theory of money that

$$P = \frac{MV}{O}$$ in which, V, velocity, and O, output, are given, so that

$$P = \gamma M,$$

it at least transforms it into the conditional proposition that an increase in the quantity of money will affect prices, as it first affects the labor market; labor-market behavior becomes the conduit by which monetary changes work their way through to price changes. Furthermore, to the extent that labor-market conditions may lead to changes in money wages that are independent of changes in the money supply, price changes are independent of money-supply changes. From this it follows that the classical view that the price level is determined by the money supply is neither reliable nor precise.

In Keynes's view of price-level determination, the marginal productivity of labor, $(d\Theta/dN)(N_E)$, decreases as employment increases, so that for a fixed wage rate the price level will rise as employment increases. In this way, the real wage of employed workers will decline with employment increases even if money wages do not change. It is important to recognize that in a capitalist economy even though bargains are struck and contracts are written in money terms, the real terms of any bargain or contract that stretches over time are determined by the way prices behave. Note that this insight—that system performance determines the real terms of contracts struck in monetary, or nominal, terms—introduces a type of uncertainty into economic decisions that is beyond the control, or guidance, of individual economic agents. It also is obvious that this principle applies not only to wage contracts but also to financial contracts.

On the other hand, if the marginal product of labor is constant for the relevant range of employment, then the price level will be constant, and we can write

$$P = \mu W$$

where μ is the "ratio" markup on wages. This is a quite common assumption.

However, in the evolution to today's neoclassical theory, the Hicks-

Hansen *IS-LM* formulation has not been integrated with the labor market in accordance with Keynes's view that labor-market behavior and labor productivity affect primarily prices. Rather, the assumption that is made in the study of competitive markets—that any enterprise will employ labor up to the point where the money wage is equal to the value of the marginal product (i.e.,

$$W_j = P_i \, \frac{d\Theta_i}{dN_j}$$

for each of the i outputs in the economy and each of the j types of labor)—is generalized into an aggregate assumption: that the number of workers employed in the economy as a whole will be such that the marginal product of a worker equals the real wage, W/P;

$$\frac{d\Theta}{dN} = \Theta_N(\bar{K}, N) = \frac{W}{P} \quad \text{so that}$$

$$N_D = \Theta^{-1}{}_N\left(\bar{K}, \frac{W}{P}\right).$$

This N_D curve is negatively sloped; in the short run, K, the capital stock, is assumed to be a constant, $\bar{K}$.

To this demand curve a supply curve is joined. This supply curve presupposes that the workers' work-leisure choice is determined by the real wage, so that

$$N_s = \xi\left(\frac{W}{P}\right), \quad \text{where} \quad N_s \text{ is the labor supply.}$$

Furthermore, $dN_s/d(W/P) > 0$; that is, this N_s curve is positively sloped.

The intersection of the N_s and N_D curves determines the equilibrium real wage and employment. In the classical economics it is blithely assumed that there exist processes in markets which assure that this real wage and employment will be achieved (see diagram 2.4). After making this assumption, employment, N_E, can be entered into the production function to yield output $O = \Theta(\bar{K}, N_E)$. This output, determined by the equilibrium conditions in the labor market, can now be "substituted" into the investment, saving, and liquidity-preference functions that make up the *IS-LM* framework, to determine a classical model that uses the Hicksian framework. In this transformation, the consumption, invest-

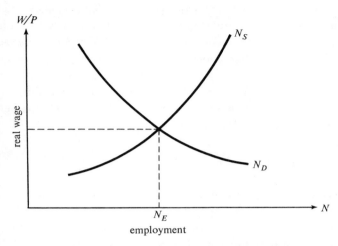

Diagram 2.4   THE CLASSICAL LABOR MARKET

ment, and liquidity-preference functions are defined in real terms. Inasmuch as the quantity of money is by definition a nominal term, the price level is explicity introduced into the liquidity-preference function, i.e.,

$$\frac{M_d}{P} = L(i,O).$$

The investment and saving functions combined into the *IS* curve of the Hicks model yield the interest rate–real income (output) combinations compatible with equilibrium in the commodity market. As the classical model assumes that output is determined by the equilibrium in the labor market, the investment and saving markets yield an interest rate.

Given that the interest rate and output are determined in the commodity and labor markets, the liquidity-preference curve has but one "assignment"; to determine the price level. Whereas in the *IS-LM* framework the liquidity-preference function states the interest rates and real income compatible with equilibrium in the money market, in the classical model the liquidity-preference relation transforms real income as determined in the labor market into money income. Liquidity preference, first transformed into a demand curve for money by Hicks, now has no function but to determine the price level. As the liquidity-preference function relates the price level to an "exogenously" determined money supply, we have arrived at a quantity theory of money. The difference between this model and the naïve $MV = PT$ formulation of the quantity theory is that velocity is a variable which depends upon the interest rate.

This model in which the labor market dominates in determining output is the classical model in modern dress. It solves each market in isolation and in a sequence. The labor market

$$N_s = \xi\left(\frac{W}{P}\right), \quad N_D = \Theta^{-1}\left(\frac{W}{P}\right), \quad \text{and } N_D = N_s$$

determines employment, and by way of the production function, real income, $\bar{O} = \Theta(\bar{K},\bar{N})$. Given income, the saving function, $S = S(i,\bar{O})$, and the investment function, $I = I(i,\bar{O})$, determine the interest rate, $\bar{i}$, and the investment-consumption division of the output pie. Given income and the interest rate, the liquidity preference function $M_D/P = L(\bar{O},\bar{i})$ together with the exogenous money supply $M_s = \bar{M}$ yields the price level. Using $M_s = M_D$, we get

$$P = \frac{\bar{M}}{L(\bar{O},\bar{i})} \quad \text{which is equivalent to} \quad P = \frac{k(\bar{i})}{\bar{O}} M.$$

The price level is determined by the quantity of money. The only sophistication over and beyond the naïve constant-velocity quantity theory is that velocity of circulation is a variable determined by the interest rate.

The equilibrium in the classical model is determined by technological conditions, as embodied in the production function, and by the preference systems of households. The production function determines the marginal-productivity functions for labor and capital, which in turn determine the demand curve for labor and the investment-demand functions. The preference systems of households in the classical system can be considered as the technology of households: it transforms leisure and saving into satisfaction. Thus the supply curves of labor and of saving are determined by transformations of the preference system in a manner analagous to the determination of demand for labor and investment.

The classical model, in which an exogenous money supply determines the price level, and the IS-LM model with a Keynesian labor market, in which an exogenous wage rate determines the price level, are constructed in parallel ways. In the classical model the labor market is dominant and determines employment and output, the saving and investment markets determine the interest rate, and the exogenously determined money supply determines the price level. In the *IS-LM* model with a Keynesian labor market, income and the interest rate are determined by the dominant simultaneous satisfaction of the equilibrium conditions in the commodity and the money markets, the income so determined yields the amount of labor employed (via the employment function), and the now determined productivity of labor, together with the exogenously determined wage rate, yields the price level.

Both the classical model and the Keynesian *IS-LM* model may be extended by making either the money supply—or its rate of change—or the rate of change of the wage rate endogenous. A money-supply function that relates changes in the quantity of money to interest rates and banking-behavior characteristics may be introduced into the classical model. A Phillips curve[12] which relates money-wage changes to unemployment rates and the rate of change of unemployment can be introduced into the Keynesian *IS-LM*-based model.

The classical model really proves too much. It makes substantial and prolonged variations in employment an accidental or a transitory phenomenon, not a systemic variable. Some way of reconciling labor-market behavior with the investment, saving, and money-market determination of aggregate demand, other than the straightforward dominance by the labor market that the classical model asserts, is necessary if observed variations in employment are to reflect systemic phenomena.

One way of reconciling the classical and the Keynesian views of labor markets is to posit a sequence of equilibria and time-consuming processes in moving toward equilibrium. In this view, observed unemployment and the reactions of the *IS-LM* framework become disequilibrium phenomena.

One way of going about the construction of a theory which treats the possibility of unemployment seriously is to wed the Hicks-Hansen determination of aggregate demand with the labor-market determination of real wages. This can be done in such a way that the demand for labor, derived from aggregate demand, in the first instance dominates the determination of employment as derived from marginal productivity and

[12] See Phillips, "The Relation between Unemployment and the Rate of Money Wage Rates in the United Kingdom, 1862–1957."

household preference considerations. Thus if income, as determined by IS-LM considerations, leads up to an excess, or a deficiency, of the demand for labor over the labor market's own "equilibrium" demand, then the dynamic movement will be to increase or decrease employment so that employment equals the demand for labor as determined by IS-LM. After this takes place, money wages may begin to change in a manner appropriate to achieving the "equilibrium" determined by the intersection of the demand for labor, derived from introducing real aggregate demand as determined by IS-LM into the production function, and the supply of labor.

In diagram 2.5, point A represents the "classical" or labor market's own equilibrium, and the lines N_{DEF} and N_{EX} reflect the demand for labor derived from the aggregate-demand-determining relations contained in the IS-LM format: N_{DEF} is a deficient and N_{EX} is an excess labor demand. In the first instance we assume that the changes, brought about by movements toward equilibrium in the labor market, do not impinge upon the markets encapsulated in the IS-LM format. Thus with N_{DEF} as

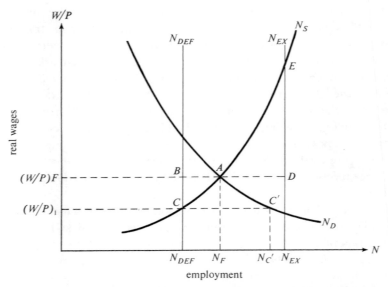

Diagram 2.5   THE LABOR MARKET WITH QUANTITY ADJUST-MENTS

the effective demand curve for labor, the new equilibrium of demand and supply will be at C, with N_{EX}, the new equilibrium will be at E.

At point C the quantity of labor demanded, as derived from the commodity and money markets, equals the quantity supplied. The commodity and money markets are in equilibrium: there are no incentives for change coming from that direction. All the workers willing to work at this real wage are employed, and there is no incentive to change from that direction. It is true that given the real wage and production functions, enterprises would like to hire C' workers, increasing employment and output. However, as enterprises canvas prospective purchasers they find that in the aggregate no market for the additional output exists. Workers' demand, determined by workers' income, N_{DEF} $(W/P)_1$, when added to investment demand is just sufficient to buy the output that N_{DEF} workers will produce. Point C, once achieved, is an equilibrium that does not satisfy the productivity conditions underlying the classical labor-demand function which, at $(W/P)_1$, leads to a labor demand C'.

Let us look at labor demand, C', in the light of the *IS-LM* framework. If real wages are $(W/P)_1$ then profit-maximizing conditions for the firm indicate that $O = \theta(K, N_C)$ should be produced. However, given the way in which demand is generated by saving, investment, and money-market conditions, there is no way in which the output produced by $N_{C'}$ workers will draw forth sufficient demand to absorb that output. The labor-market position as indicated by point C, even though it is a labor-market disequilibrium as defined by the classical conditions, does not by itself trigger a dynamic process which tends to eliminate the excess demand $(C'-C)$ for labor. The excess demand $(C'-C)$ is notional, not effective. All that is required for the situation at C to be sustainable is that the income of enterprises be sufficient to meet various financial commitments; that is, that entrepreneurs do not go bankrupt when the economy is at C. Once this sufficient financial condition is satisfied, there is no endogenous disturbing influence.

In principle, point C, being on the supply curve of labor, is a full-employment equilibrium. However, the memory that in that past employment was N_F, that past output was greater than present output, and that past profits were greater than present profits will lead to this equilibrium being identified as a less than satisfactory state of the economy. Point C, while not characterizing a deep depression, might very well characterize an economy in recession, or one that is stagnant or sluggish.

If labor demand, as derived from output demand determined in the commodity and money markets, exceeds the full-employment equilibrium, then there will be a tendency for employment and the real wage to rise. Let us assume that point E is achieved. At point E labor supply, commodity market, and money market equilibrium conditions are all "met." However, at this output the marginal productivity of labor is lower than the real wage, and presumably there is an incentive to cut output and employment. Will this incentive result in a restriction of output? Once again, we assume that changes in the labor market do not affect aggregate demand and that the incomes of enterprises are sufficient to meet their various financial commitments.

For output to be reduced, it is necessary to assume that firms making adequate overall profits will turn away orders and will cut production, even though on the margin the firm takes losses on the last units of sales. Appealing to "factual" considerations, a firm is loath to turn away customers today if it endangers their custom tomorrow. Furthermore, if firms are in the situation exemplified by point E, they will be engaged in investment programs that will lead to a rise in capacity—which would enable them to satisfy the demand which now leads to N_{EX}—at a labor productivity that is higher than now rules.

Admittedly, the argument that points C and E are less than and more than full-employment equilibria involves a bit of hand waving. Nevertheless, the big hole in the argument does not center around what happens if the economy is at point C or E, but rather around whether these points are attainable: whether the processes set up by a shift of labor demand from, say, N_F to N_{DEF} will achieve an equilibrium at C. The disequilibrium process has two facets: one, the own-market reactions, and the second a feedback to the LM and IS curves of the Hicks-Hansen framework. Once the IS or the LM curves are affected, the question arises whether this leads to an appropriate (equilibrating) shift in the N_{DEF} or the N_{EX} curves. That is, if the own-market dynamics cannot move the economy from an initial disequilibrium to a full equilibrium, can this be accomplished by a dynamics which incorporates interactions among markets?

FULL EQUILIBRIUM: THE NEOCLASSICAL SYNTHESIS

A key contribution of Keynes to the study of disequilibrium processes is the explicit introduction of the perspective that changes induced by disequilibrium in a particular market may have their major effect upon the initially affected market by first affecting conditions in other markets; that is, the reaction to a disequilibrium in one market may induce disequilibria in other markets. The question arises whether these intermarket feedbacks lead to a new equilibrium or whether the feedback process exacerbates the initial disequilibrium.

In an isolated minor market of price theory, an excess of quantity supplied over that demanded at a particular price will lead to a fall in price in that market. Such a price decline will be equilibrating in its own market and have no perceptible effect on other markets. This perspective is the rationalization for partial equilibrium analysis. The classical model treats the labor market in this way even though, in an aggregate market, such as the labor market, the price and quantity changes set up by a disequilibrium are likely to have significant effects in other markets. The impact of own-market changes on other markets and the feedbacks from other markets to the initial market will, in combination with the own-market reactions, determine the path of the system.

Starting from an initial equilibrium at point *A* in diagram 2.5, a short-fall of demand will initially decrease employment at a given wage, and the movement will be to point *B*. In what follows we will take up the case of a shortfall in demand; a symmetrical argument follows if an excess of demand is the initial condition. At this point we must recognize that the wage in a capitalist economy is a money wage rather than the real wage. Let us assume that the deficit of demand triggers a fall in money wages. But the price level is given by money wages divided by productivity: prices will tend to fall with wages.

Money wages enter price determination two ways—as a cost and as an income. The lowering of money wages will tend to increase the quantity of output employers are willing to supply at any price, but the lowering of money wages will also lower the amount employed workers can buy at any price level. Starting a wage deflation can be a treadmill insofar as real wages are concerned. The price level and money wages will change in the same direction and in essentially the same ratio. A money-wage deflation may be an inefficient way of rectifying any disequilibrium in real wages and employment by way of own-market reactions: once the movement to the employment level given by point *B* in diagram 2.5 takes place, the economy may be stuck there.

However, a fall in money wages and the price level will affect the real value of money—where the quantity of money is fixed in nominal terms—as well as of debts. If money is mainly the deposit liability of banks, then money may to a very large extent be offset by the private debt holdings of banks (this is called inside money). For every real gain to a holder of money by way of price fall, there is real loss to some debtor on the assets owned by the bank. The increase in the real burden of private debt as the price level falls is an inducement for private parties to decrease their debt. In this way a process which entails declines in money wages and money prices will be associated with decreases in the amount of nominal money—especially if the money supply is mainly of the inside variety. Only if we assume that the behavior of bank creditors is affected and the behavior of bank debtors is not by these changes in the real value of their assets or debts can it be assured that wage and price-level movement which tend to increase the quantity of bank money as deflated by the price level will tend to affect demand.

However, there is a part of the money supply which is not offset by private debts to a bank: specie as coin and as bank reserves; treasury currency; and finally, treasury debts of various kinds owned by banks and even, by extension, treasury debt owned by private parties. (Coin, treasury currency, and treasury debt are called outside money.) In a price deflation the real value of these assets rises.

This increase in the real value of privately held money that is not offset by a private debt is a way in which the labor-market disequilibrium affects other markets, and thus affects the equilibrium represented by the *IS-LM* diagram underlying the labor-market diagram.

One way in which the increased real value of money will affect the *IS-LM* markets is by increasing the real quantity of money in the *LM* diagram, i.e., by shifting *LM* to the right. If the liquidity trap is not ruling this will tend to lower interest rates, which in turn may increase investment and thus income. This is sometimes called the "Keynes" effect: it may lead to an "equilibrating" shift of the labor-demand function toward the equilibrium defined by the "classical" intersection of the labor demand and supply curves.

This process, however, may be inefficient. One objection to the argument which is true for any speculative demand is that the falling price level can set up expectations that the price level will continue to fall. This can lead to an expectation that investment-goods prices which are falling will continue to fall. Since entrepreneurs in a situation characterized by N_{DEF} have not only a potential excess supply of labor but an actual excess supply of capital equipment, they are in a good position to put off ordering investment goods during such a deflationary process. Thus, at least initially, any process which depends upon investment ordering for the expansion of demand may not be triggered when excess supply rules.

A feature of the data on consumption that emerged in the late 1930s and early 1940s is that even though cyclical consumption data seem to show a decreasing average propensity to consume, secular consumption data indicate that the consumption-income ratio has been essentially constant. An explanation of this constant average propensity to consume that has emerged is that real wealth has grown along with income, and that this growth in real wealth offsets the increases in the saving ratio that would otherwise accompany rising incomes. This has been interpreted as indicating that the short-run or cyclical consumption function drifts upward as accumulation takes place. By assuming that an increase in nominal wealth has the same effect as a rise in real wealth, we posit an upward-drifting consumption function as deflation increases the real purchasing power of outside money and financial assets. This effect of the purchasing power of monetary assets upon consumption is called the "real balance" effect. The assumption which is fundamental to the neoclassical synthesis holds that an increase in paper wealth, as deflation takes place, is as potent as an increase in real wealth by accumulation in decreasing desired saving out of income. This price deflation effect will shift the IS curve to the right in the (L,Y) plane, raising aggregate demand.

Thus a price deflation has two effects upon aggregate demand that tend to increase demand and one that tends to decrease demand. A deflation will raise the real quantity of money, thereby lowering interest rates; it will raise the real purchasing power of appropriate monetary wealth, thus decreasing saving; and it will decrease investment by way of the impact of deflationary expectations. In principle, the potential decrease in investment is limited—there is a maximum rate of disinvestment for any level of use of capital equipment. Furthermore, the explicit consideration of destabilizing expectations is foreign to the spirit of the neoclassical synthesis. Because of the liquidity trap, the impact upon interest rates of increasing the quantity of money may also be of limited potency. However, the potential impact of lower prices upon saving is unlimited. In principle, the saving function can be so "placed" by this process that all or more than all of full-employment income will be consumed. Therefore, the introduction of the real quantity of money into the saving function makes it certain that the employment function as derived from the inverse of the aggregate-supply function can be "forced" to pass through the intersection of the classical labor demand and labor supply functions (point *A* in diagram 2.5). Equilibrium at full employment is guaranteed by the deflation process. Furthermore, unemployment can persist only if unemployment does not trigger a fall in money wages; that is, money wages are sticky.

The equilibrium derived by shifting the saving function so that labor demand, as determined by inverting the aggregate-supply function, equals the equilibrium employment in the labor market is a full equilibrium, in the sense that all the functions of the *IS-LM* model are satisfied at the same time as the labor-market conditions are satisfied. If the initial "shock" out of a full equilibrium to an unemployment situation is due to a change in the money supply (either the money supply is all outside money, or it is a mixed inside-outside money supply in which the inside and the outside components change in the same proportion), then the results of the price deflation that returns the system to full employment will be neutral—that is, all the real values of the system will be unchanged—and the quantity-theory result that prices change in proportion to the money supply will obtain.

The demonstration that the economy will reach the classical "technologically" determined full-employment equilibrium by way of price deflation if unemployment exists is not taken to mean, by those who have developed these models, that this should be the chosen policy instrument. Within this argument, the possibility remains that monetary and fiscal policy can rectify the deficit in aggregate demand more expeditiously than the price-deflation process. Even though in principle the system is self-equilibrating, the automatic path may be too hard to take: it might take too long, or it may be inoperative because of wage rigidities. Thus positive Keynesian fiscal and monetary policy may be desirable even though in principle it is not necessary: the neoclassical synthesis permits the advocacy of an active full-employment policy to be consistent with an in-theory belief in the self-equilibrating nature of the economy. Although Keynes has been, so to speak, defeated as a scientist and as an economic theorist, the view from the neoclassical synthesis is that he may have carried the field as a wise man who has written in a useful and valid fashion about economic policy.

CONCLUSION

The journey through various standard models that embody elements derived from *The General Theory* has led us to the position that such Keynesian models are either trivial (the consumption-function models), incomplete (the *IS-LM* models without a labor market), inconsistent (the *IS-LM* models with a labor market but no real-balance effect), or indistinguishable in their results from those of the older quantity-theory models (the neoclassical synthesis). True, the equilibrating process for the neoclassical synthesis involves simultaneous and interacting changes in various markets. The neoclassical synthesis is not naïve, for labor-market equilibrium is not posited and the full-employment output so determined is not fed into the saving, investment, and money relations. Because the process of moving from an initial nonequilibrium position to an equilibrium position involves intermarket reactions, it may be slow, and at various points the markets, perhaps for institutional reasons, might not react or might react in a disequilibrating fashion. In particular a sluggish, or rigid, labor market—due perhaps to the existence of trade-union power—may prevent an excess supply of labor from leading to a fall in money wages. Thus wage rigidity is held to be responsible for unemployment; involuntary unemployment disappears in the neoclassical world.

This pointing at labor-market sluggishness or rigidity with respect to money wages as the villian of the piece contrasts with Keynes's view that wage flexibility, if it occurred, might very well make things worse. Keynes's view was not based solely upon the speculative nature of investment demand, although he recognized that this was a factor mitigating against the efficacy of wage deflation. He also considered the process by which inside money is generated in the banking system. Falling wages, prices, and cash flows to enterprises will make the burden of debt to potential bank borrowers increase over the life of the loan. A decline in wages and prices will tend to set off a money-decreasing, debt-deflation process, which will exacerbate the initial deficit of demand for labor—that is, wage and price-level flexibility is disequilibrating.

We have now carried the standard approaches built upon Keynes as far as we need; we will now turn to the neglected or lost facets of *The General Theory* and show how they lead to quite a different view of the capitalist process.

‹ 3 ›

Fundamental
Perspectives

INTRODUCTION

Today's dominant interpretation as embodied in the neo-classical synthesis holds that Keynes's *The General Theory* presents an equilibrium model not truly different from that which would have been accepted by a sophisticated follower of Marshall at the time Keynes wrote. In this view, if what is taken to be Keynes's main unconventional proposition—that enduring underemployment is a possible state of a capitalist economy—is true, it is because either rigidities, especially of money wages, or particular shapes of functional relations, such as the liquidity trap, are assumed to be empirically valid. A standard view is that the neoclassical synthesis, achieved when the real-balance effect was introduced into a Keynesian framework to assure that the simultaneous equilibrium in the commodity and money markets would be consistent with labor-market equilibrium, was implicit in the pre-Keynesian argu-ments. Once this real-balance effect has been introduced, standard the-ory shows that the market mechanism is not inherently flawed: market processes will achieve and sustain full employment.

Furthermore, if unemployment develops and persists, because of rigidities, institutional weaknesses, or policy errors, standard theory holds that two paths are available for policy. Along one, the wise use of monetary and fiscal policy will offset the barriers to full equilibrium or the errors that led to unemployment. Along the other, changes in the structural characteristics of the economy may be effected, so as to remove the rigidities and institutional shortcomings that cause lapses from full employment to occur and persist.

In this neoclassical view Keynes's enduring contribution lies mainly in the arena of public policy: his arguments made it intellectually respectable to advocate activist intervention to guide the economy. It is also held that once the fact that some adjustment processes are sluggish is taken into account, intervention of an aggregate nature, i.e., monetary and fiscal policy, was implicit in the presumably laissez-faire-oriented classical economics.

This interpretation of his argument was explicitly repudiated by Keynes in his rebuttal to Viner's review. Viner contended that "in modern monetary theory the propensity to hoard is generally dealt with, with results which in kind are substantially identical with Keynes', as a factor operating to reduce the 'velocity' of money."[1] In Viner's view, Keynes's theory is essentially the Marshallian model with the addition of a precise specification of how velocity is determined. Hicks's interpretation of *The General Theory* in "Mr. Keynes and the 'Classics,' " where he states that "his [Keynes's] theory becomes hard to distinguish from the revised and qualified Marshallian theories which, as we have seen, are not new"[2] is similar to Viner's.

Keynes's rejection of Viner's interpretation is unambiguous. He wrote "I cannot agree with Viner's interpretation"; and furthermore, he was "convinced that the monetary theorists who try to deal with it [the demand for money] in this [Viner's] way are altogether on the wrong track" (*QJE*, p. 211).

In this and the next four chapters, we will put forth an interpretation of *The General Theory* that is an alternative to the one which led to the neoclassical synthesis. This alternative is consistent with the views expressed by Keynes in his rebuttal to Viner. The alternative interpretation emphasizes that Keynes constructed a theory to explain the behavior

[1] Viner, "Mr. Keynes on the Causes of Unemployment," p. 152.
[2] Hicks, "Mr. Keynes and the 'Classics,' " p. 153.

of a capitalist economy which is sophisticated in its financial institutions. Such an economy is inherently flawed, because it is intractably cyclical—that is, such a capitalist economy cannot by its own processes sustain full employment, and each of a succession of cyclical states is transitory in the sense that relations are built up which transform the way in which the economy will behave.

A capitalist economy is characterized by private ownership of the means of production and private investment. In a sophisticated capitalist economy, monetary and financial institutions determine the way in which the funds required both for the ownership of items in the stock of capital assets and for the production of new capital assets are obtained. In a capitalist economy of the kind that Keynes postulated, there are private portfolios, real-capital assets are in essential details equivalent to speculative financial assets, and banks, generically defined as institutions specializing in finance, are important. In Keynes's theory the proximate cause of the transitory nature of each cyclical state is the instability of investment; but the deeper cause of business cycles in an economy with the financial institutions of capitalism is the instability of portfolios and of financial interrelations.

In the part of *The General Theory* that was lost to standard economics as it evolved into the neoclassical synthesis, Keynes put forth an investment theory of fluctuations in real demand and a financial theory of fluctuations in real investment. Desired portfolio composition and thus financial relations in general are most clearly the areas of decision where changing views about the future can most quickly affect current behavior. This responsiveness is true not only for ultimate units like business firms and households but also for specifically financial institutions like commercial banks, investment banks, etc. But the future is uncertain. To understand Keynes it is necessary to understand his sophisticated view about uncertainty, and the importance of uncertainty in his vision of the economic process. Keynes without uncertainty is something like *Hamlet* without the Prince.

In this chapter we will take up three perspectives about the nature of what is being studied that are fundamental to interpreting and understanding Keynes. These are the cyclical environment, uncertainty, and the nature of investment. Whereas classical economics and the neoclassical synthesis are based upon a barter paradigm—the image is of a yeoman or a craftsman trading in a village market—Keynesian theory rests upon a speculative-financial paradigm—the image is of a banker making his deals on a Wall Street.

In the next four chapters these perspectives are used to derive a Keynesian theory of investment and system behavior. This theory emphasizes the financial and speculative determinants of what happens.

THE BUSINESS-CYCLE PERSPECTIVE

In explaining why he cannot accept Viner's interpretation of liquidity preference, Keynes argues from a business-cycle framework. He begins his argument with the phrase, "When, as happens in a crisis . . ." (*QJE*, p. 211). As Professor Joan Robinson put it, rigidities were not the explanation of unemployment:

> Keynes' argument was not the one that has been foisted on him by the bastard Keynesians—that money-wage rates are rigid for institutional reasons. It was that if wages could be cut, in a slump, it would make the situation worse. . . .[3]

The evidence that it is legitimate to interpret *The General Theory* as dealing with an economy that is cyclical by reason of its essential institutions is spread throughout the volume. References to cyclical phenomena occur not only in chapter 22 of *The General Theory*, "Notes on the Trade Cycle," which explicitly deals with business cycles, and in the rebuttal to Viner in *The Quarterly Journal of Economics* of February 1937, but throughout his book. When *The General Theory* is read from the perspective that the subject matter is a sophisticated capitalist economy, whose past and whose future entail business cycles, the ratifying references for an interpretation within a cyclical context are everywhere evident. In the preface Keynes wrote:

> This book . . . has evolved into what is primarily a study of the forces which determine changes in the scale of output and employment as a whole. . . . A monetary economy . . . is essentially one in which changing views about the future are capable of influencing the quantity of employment and not merely its direction. [*GT*, p. vii]

The first paragraph of chapter 22 reads:

> Since we claim to have shown in the preceding chapters what determines the volume of employment at any time, it follows that if we are right, that our theory must be capable of explaining the phenomena of the Trade Cycle. [*GT*, p. 313]

[3] Robinson, *Economic Heresies*, pp. 90–91; emphasis added.

Similarly, as Keynes finishes his reply to Viner he writes, "This that I offer is, therefore, a theory of why output and employment are so liable to fluctuation" (*QJE*, p. 221).

In 1936, when *The General Theory* appeared, the world was in the seventh year of the Great Depression. Although a considerable recovery from the low point of 1933 had taken place, and the series of financial traumas and crises that marked the years between 1929 and 1933 were now apparently past, unemployment rates remained high. In the United States the peak national incomes of the late 1920s had not yet been regained. The world economy was sluggish and stagnant, the spirit of enterprise, though alive, was not vigorous.

The standard economic theory of the time—what Keynes called the "classical" school—had failed to predict the coming of the depression, to understand why it took place, to explain its depth and duration, or to offer useful guidance to policy.[4] From the point of view of the standard economic theory of 1930s, the events in the United States in the period 1929–33 were unexplainable. Keynes took these current events as his point of departure: his new view was going to make the anomaly the ordinary.

Obviously, economists (both classical and deviant), publicists, and politicians had offered explanations of the great contraction as it occurred. Overinvestment, underconsumption, overindebtedness, a hangover from a speculative orgy, the fractional-reserve banking system, Central Bank errors, trade unions (virtually nonexistent in the United States), worker resistance to wage cuts, low farm prices, and a failure of confidence were offered by both scholars and pundits as explanations of the Great Depression. Each one-dimensional explanation was easily exploded; precise descriptions of business-cycle states and processes did exist, but they were not integrated into an overall analytical system.

Keynes put forth in *The General Theory* a model capable of explaining each cyclical state of an economy. This model combined aspects of the

---

[4]As was mentioned earlier, some economists trained in the classical theory were offering what would now be considered valid policy advice during the Great Depression, while others were offering what would now be considered nonsense. However, the valid advice was based upon intuition and observations (or good sense), not upon any integrated theory. Whether the economists offering good advice constituted a minority or a majority of the leading classical economists is irrelevant. Their valid advice was inconsistent with their proclaimed theory, and they were unable to offer persuasive arguments for the validity of their advice.

various one-dimensional-cycle explanations into a multidimensional, integrated analytical structure:

> If we examine the details of any actual instance of the Trade Cycle, we shall find that it is highly complex and that every element in our analysis will be required for its complete explanation. In particular we shall find that fluctuations in the propensity to consume, in the state of liquidity preference and in the marginal efficiency of capital have all played a part. [*GT*, p. 313]

The underconsumption thrust of cycle theorizing was encompassed by the consumption function, overindebtedness and imperfections of the monetary system were taken care of by liquidity preference, and the overinvestment theme was embodied in the marginal-efficiency-of capital schedule. In addition, the state of confidence, which was represented by a sophisticated discussion of uncertainty and expectations, was integrated into the theory as a determinant of position, as a "parameter of shift" of the other functions. Various price-rigidity arguments were taken into account by recognizing the relative sluggishness of wages and other costs, so that the natural "numeraire," or fixed point, in price-level determination was the money-wage rate.

The General Theory is not a theory of the business cycle as such, but rather it is a theory of how the current transitory state of an economy is determined and how the robustness of these transitory states is undermined. Each current state results from interactions among an unchanging set of market forces as represented by the shape and position of a small number of fundamental functional relations. Furthermore, if we ignore the introduction of uncertainty, which was never formalized to the same extent as the other functional relations, it is possible to put each of the novel functions Keynes introduced into a form that is similar, or analogous, to a relation that appears in the formal versions of classical models. That is, once uncertainty and the cyclical perspective were ignored, which is a tall order, the new theory could be phrased in terms of familiar constructs, first modified and then put together in a novel manner.

However, the concepts which it is usual to ignore or deemphasize in interpreting Keynes, the cyclical perspective, the relations between investment and finance, and uncertainty, are the keys to an understanding of the full significance of his contribution. Perhaps one reason why the Keynesian Revolution was aborted is that the new ideas were stated within a framework that utilized many of the traditional theoretical constructs; and perhaps the traditional constructs were used because Keynes himself had not fully escaped from the "habitual modes of thought and expression" of which he warned in his preface (*GT*, p. viii). One point made in the argument that will follow is that the assumption that a negatively sloped marginal-efficiency-of-capital schedule existed tended to obscure the significance of uncertainty and financial market variables in the investment process. In particular, the phrasing of the price level of capital assets in terms of interest rates muddled his message with respect to the determinants of investment.

The functional relations of *The General Theory* generate each of the short-period positions, which were identified as equilibria. By its very nature, a short-run equilibrium is transitory. In the Marshallian short-run equilibrium in a particular market, capital accumulation or decumulation is going on, so that in time, and if the process is uninterrupted, the capital-stock conditions for long-run equilibrium will be satisfied. In the Marshallian long-run equilibrium there are no endogenous economic forces making for further change. Exogenous population changes, innovations, and institutional changes, as well as political developments, may affect the long-run equilibrium toward which the system is tending and shake the economy out of equilibrium, but the Marshallian vision is that of a system tending toward rest.

Every reference by Keynes to an equilibrium is best interpreted as a reference to a transitory set of system variables toward which the economy is tending; but, in contrast to Marshall, as the economy moves toward such a set of system variables, endogenously determined changes occur which affect the set of system variables toward which the economy tends. The analogy is that a moving target, which is never achieved but for a fleeting instant, if at all. Each state, whether it be boom, crisis, debt-deflation, stagnation, or expansion, is transitory. During each short-period equilibrium, in Keynes's view, processes are at work which will "disequilibrate" the system. Not only is stability an unattainable goal; whenever something approaching stability is achieved, destabilizing processes are set off.

Keynes did not construct a simple two-state (short-run and long-run) equilibrium model, such as Marshall's. In Keynes's model the system is capable of being in one of a number of states, each of which carries the seeds of its own destruction. Among the system states we can distinguish are boom, crisis, deflation, stagnation, expansion, and recovery. Each of these system states is mentioned in *The General Theory* and each is related to a preceding and a succeeding system state. Each system state is characterized by the shape (elasticity) and position of the various functions. However there is no precise treatment of the boom, crisis, deflation, and expansion states in *The General Theory*. These system states are heavily determined by financial behavior, and the financial details of the economy, while hinted at, are not thoroughly or systemically investigated.

These are only some of the dimensions of the problems taken up in *The General Theory* and in Keynes's rebuttal to Viner which have been ignored in the standard exegeses and developments of Keynesian economics. As a result, standard Keynesian economics is a truncated two-stage affair in which the less-than-full-employment equilibrium of a stagnant state leads, with a longer or a shorter lag, to a full-employment equilibrium. Inasmuch as the less-than-full-employment state was both the "novel" state explored in *The General Theory*, and especially relevant to the then ruling world situation, the erroneous view that "The General Theory of Employment is the Economics of Depression"[5] became quite generally accepted.

The cyclical succession of system states is not always clearly presented in *The General Theory*. In fact, there are two distinct views of the business cycle, one a moderate cycle which can perhaps be identified with a dampened accelerator-multiplier cycle and the second a vigorous "boom and bust" cycle. In chapter 18 (*GT*, pp. 249–54) Keynes sketches a model of a moderate business cycle that might very well be the prototype for the various nonexplosive accelerator-multiplier interaction models. The business cycle as described is based upon a modest multiplier and a moderately fluctuating prospective yield of investment. This investment-multiplier model is viewed as

adequate to explain the outstanding features of our actual experience;—namely, that we oscillate, avoiding the gravest extremes of fluctuation in employment and in prices in both directions, round an intermediate position appreciably below full employment and appreciably above the minimum employment a decline below which would endanger life. [*GT*, p. 254]

The business cycle in chapter 18 does not exhibit booms or crises.

In chapters 12 and 22, in the rebuttal to Viner, and in remarks throughout *The General Theory*, a vigorous cycle, which does have booms

[5]Hicks, "Mr. Keynes and the 'Classics,' " p. 155.

and crises, is described. However, nowhere in *The General Theory* or in Keynes's few post–General Theory articles explicating his new theory are the boom and the crisis adequately defined or explained. The financial developments during a boom that make a crisis likely, if not inevitable, are hinted at but not thoroughly examined. This is the logical hole, the missing link, in *The General Theory* as it was left by Keynes in 1937 after his rebuttal to Viner. The interpretive tradition that leads to today's standard macroeconomics abstracted from the financial detail and thus from the system states that are most heavily financial in their character—the boom, the crisis, and the debt-deflation. In order to appreciate the full potential of *The General Theory* as a guide to the interpretation and understanding of modern capitalism, we must fill out what Keynes discussed in a fragmentary and casual manner. Even though booms and crises were not studied in a systematic manner in *The General Theory*, they are key elements for our understanding of Keynes's argument.

The absence of an explicit and precise discussion of the details of booms and crises by Keynes should not really deter us from taking up this task. In the early 1930s, when *The General Theory* was conceived, the great crash in Wall Street was in the minds of all; explicit, continuing discussion of the great crash was not necessary in order to make one's point.

After World War I, in good part because of the inappropriate return of the pound to its prewar parity (which, as is well known, Keynes opposed), Britain entered into a period of chronic unemployment and stagnation in its mines and mills. This 1920s stagnation was easily explicable within the classical tradition by the incongruence between the domestic price level in pounds and the dollar price of pound goods as determined by the exchange rate. The 1920s' stagnation in Britain did not give rise to a need for a new theory; all that was necessary in order to make the old theory suffice was a recognition that wages and the composition of industry adjusted slowly to circumstances that had changed radically. In fact, with the pound devaluation in 1931, Britain enjoyed a bit of a "boomlet" in spite of the developing great worldwide depression. The stagnation of the 1920s could well be explained within the old doctrines; Keynes's "The Economic Consequences of Mr. Churchill,"[6] in which he discusses the return of the pound to its prewar parity, is in the classical tradition.

[6]Keynes, *Essays in Persuasion*, pp. 202–30.

Thus the anomaly which brought forth the new theory was the great crash in Wall Street and what followed. The gestation period of *A Treatise on Money* was the era of Britain's chronic stagnation; *A Treatise on Money* is within the classical tradition. The gestation period of *The General Theory* was the time of the Great Depression, which was triggered by a crisis followed by a debt-deflation process, first in the United States and then world wide. However, Keynes offered no explanation or theory of the crisis. In order to complete the picture we have to fill that hole: Keynes's theory is incomplete without a model of the endogenous generation of booms, crises, and debt deflations.[7]

UNCERTAINTY

The description of uncertainty and the process of decision-making under conditions of uncertainty were long-standing intellectual interests of Keynes. He worked on his *A Treatise on Probability*, which was published in 1921, on and off for fifteen years. *A Treatise on Probability* deals with "arguments that . . . are rational and claim some weight without pretending to be certain."[8] Furthermore, he argues there that there are "various degrees of rational belief about a proposition which different amounts of knowledge authorize us to entertain."[9] In this work Keynes differentiates between the probability of a proposition and the weight attached to a proposition; for example:

As the relevant evidence at our disposal increases, the magnitudes of the probability of the argument may either decrease or increase, according as the knowledge strengthens the unfavorable or the favorable evidence, but something seems to have increased in either case . . . as accession of new evidence increases the weight of an argument.[10]

Keynes's view in *A Treatise on Probability* was that the degree of rational belief, or probability, attached to a proposition, *a*, was conditional upon the evidence, *b*; a probability proposition is written as *a/b*. Al-

---

[7]We can assume that the general thrust of Irving Fisher's description in the "Debt-Deflation Theory of Great Depression" of the aftermath of a crisis was accepted by Keynes as a rough-and-ready statement of postcrisis system behavior, and that it was assumed implicitly that a symmetric development occurred during a boom. Fisher also failed to offer an explanation or theory of the crisis.

[8]Keynes, *A Treatise on Probability*, p. 3.

[9]Ibid.

[10]Ibid., p. 77.

though for some simple cases, such as the events that take place at a fair gaming table, a/b can be assigned a precise numerical value by understanding the objective circumstances, so that $0 \leq a/b \leq 1$, in other cases, more prevalent in the world and more relevant to economics, objective criteria, which can be fully agreed upon by sophisticated observers, do not lead to any such precise numerical value. Nevertheless, in cases where no precise numerical value can be objectively assigned, decisions need to be made. They are made as if some objective assignment of probability could be made; we might call such assigned probabilities in the absence of sufficient knowledge "subjective probabilities." Such subjective probabilities, assigned on the basis of insufficient knowledge, are subject to quick and substantial changes; thus processes due to decisions based upon such estimates can change both rapidly and markedly.

In Keynes's view, in addition to the probability assigned to a conditional proposition either on objective or subjective grounds, there is another subjective factor which intervenes in decision-making. This is the weight or confidence with which the assigned probability is used as a guide to action or decision. In *A Treatise on Probability* Keynes viewed an accretion of evidence as increasing the weight or confidence attached to a proposition. But in the context of the economic problems discussed in *The General Theory* of decision-making for the future by households, firms, and banks, events, such as crises, can radically diminish the confidence with which views of the world are held. Emerging events can both change subjective-probability distributions assigned to future events and increase or decrease the confidence with which views are held.

Whether the dual-decision scheme that Keynes advanced in *A Treatise on Probability*—subjective estimates of the relevant probabilities and an independent assignment of weights to the evidence—is an apt way of formulating decision-making under uncertainty is not essential for the argument. Perhaps this problem can be better handled by some alternative scheme—such as assuming variable subjective-probability distributions and changing preference functions with respect to uncertainty. What is essential, even fundamental, to any interpretation of Keynes is to recognize that Keynes came to the problems of economic choice that involve time (and thus uncertainty), and the behavior of an economy in which such choices are important, with a sophisticated philosophical framework for examining decisions that are made on the basis of imperfect knowledge, and that this intellectual framework permeated his economics. In addition, Keynes held that there was no way of replacing this uncertainty with certainty equivalents, and furthermore that the relevant probabilistic propositions and the weight attached to such propositions change, not in a random or unpredictable manner, but in a consistent manner in response to events.

Decision-making under uncertainty, which Keynes had treated in his *A Treatise on Probability*, is central to *The General Theory*. In his rebuttal to Viner, Keynes went to great lengths to distinguish his views about uncertainty from those of his teachers and colleagues—Marshall, Edgeworth, and Pigou. He characterized their views as holding that

at any given time facts and expectations were assumed to be given in a definite and calculable form; and risks, of which, tho admitted, not much notice was taken, were supposed to be capable of an exact actuarial computation. The calculus of probability, tho mention of it was kept in the background, was supposed to be capable of reducing uncertainty to the same calculable status as that of certainty itself.[*QJE*, p. 212–13]

Keynes then defined what he meant by "uncertain" knowledge:

By "uncertain" knowledge, let me explain, I do not mean merely to distinguish what is known for certain from what is only probable. The game of roulette is not subject, in this sense, to uncertainty; nor is the prospect of a Victory bond being drawn. Or again, the expectation of life is only slightly uncertain. Even the weather is only moderately uncertain. The sense in which I am using the term is that in which the prospect of a European war is uncertain, or the price of copper and the rate of interest twenty years hence, or the obsolescence of a new invention, or the position of private wealth owners in the social system in 1970. About these matters there is no scientific basis on which to form any calculable probability whatever. We simply do not know. Nevertheless, the necessity for action and for decision compels us as practical men to do our best to overlook this awkward fact and to behave exactly as we should if we had behind us a good Benthamite calculation of a series of prospective advantages and disadvantages, each multiplied by its appropriate probability waiting to be summed. [*QJE*, pp. 213–14]

Thus the use of certainty equivalents—much beloved by academics— is to practical men a convention, to which lip service may be paid, but which is abandoned when evidence inconsistent with the polite convention emerges.

In the face of uncertainty and "the necessity for action and for decision" (*QJE*, p. 214), we devise conventions: we assume that the present is a "serviceable guide to the future," we assume that existing market conditions are good guides to future markets, and "we endeavor to conform with the behavior of the majority or the average" (*QJE*, p. 214). Given these flimsy foundations, the view of the future "is subject to sudden and violent changes" (*QJE*, pp. 214–15). "All these pretty, polite techniques made for a well-paneled Board Room and a nicely regulated market, are liable to collapse" (*QJE*, p. 215).

Thus it is uncertainty that intervenes and attenuates the significance of the production functions and stable preference functions of conventional theory as determinants of system behavior. Uncertainty enters strongly into the determination of behavior at two points: in the portfolio decisions of households, firms, and financial institutions, and in views held by firms, by the owners of capital assets, and by the bankers to firms as to the prospective yields of capital assets.

In interpreting *The General Theory* it should be kept in mind that Keynes was first the author of *A Treatise on Probability*.

INVESTMENT AND DISEQUILIBRIUM

In Keynes's rebuttal to Viner, effective demand, which fluctuates, is made up of two components: consumption and investment. The "output of consumption goods which it pays to produce . . . is related by the multiplier formula . . . to the output of investment goods" (*QJE*, p. 220), so that "The Theory can be summed up by saying that given the psychology of the public, the level of output and employment as a whole depends upon the amount of investment" (*QJE*, p. 221). Keynes's theory is an investment theory of the cycle, in which consumption is treated initially as determining a passive amplifier, so that aggregate fluctuations are determined by investment fluctuations.

The scale of investment will fluctuate for

reasons quite distinct (*a*) from those which determine the propensity of the individual to *save* out of a given income and (*b*) from those physical conditions of technical capacity to aid production which have usually been supposed hither to be the chief influence governing the marginal efficiency of capital. [*QJE*, p. 218]

The variations in the pace of investment, which are the proximate causes of fluctuations, are not due to variations in the technical productivity of capital or in the thriftiness of households. Even if technical productivity and thriftiness were well defined and stable, investment would still be liable to fluctuations.

The "reasons quite distinct" revolve around portfolio preferences, financing conditions, and uncertainty. Keynesian economics differs from neoclassical economics in that it integrates into a model of system behavior the uncertainty inherent in a decentralized capitalist economy —where each household and, more importantly, each business firm (including banks and other financial institutions) makes intertemporal portfolio as well as contemporaneous income decisions. As a result of allowing explicitly for time, the significance of the production function in determining the output, investment, and income-distribution characteristics of the economy, as well as the significance of the idea of equilibrium, is diminished.

To Keynes the subjective evaluation of prospects over a time horizon is the major proximate basis for investment and portfolio decisions, and these subjective estimates are changeable. First of all, "Business men play a mixed game of skill and chance, the average results of which to the players are not known by those who take a hand" (*GT*, p. 150). Nevertheless, businessmen and wealth owners must make decisions. As a result of the effect on behavior of the need to make decisions under conditions of imperfect knowledge, investment by business can be volatile even though production relations are stable. The effects of uncertainty upon desired portfolios and of evolving portfolios upon desired portfolios can be such that the equilibrium toward which the system tends not only is always changing but can change rapidly. Thus the behavior of the economy is characterized by equilibrating tendencies rather than by any achieved equilibrium. Keynesian economics as the economics of disequilibrium is the economics of permanent disequilibrium.

‹ 4 ›

Capitalist Finance and the Pricing of Capital Assets

INTRODUCTION

Uncertainty most directly affects the performance of a capitalist economy by affecting the financial structure, as exemplified by the interrelated portfolios of the various units. By its very nature, a portfolio, which consists of assets owned or controlled and liabilities put out to achieve this ownership and control, involves the existence of decision units in a present position which reflects current and past views about the prospects of particular units, as well as of the economy. Keynes discusses how financial relations affect demand in Book Four of *The General Theory*, "The Inducement to Invest." Unfortunately, his discussion of finance and portfolios, and how they relate to the pricing of capital assets and the pace of investment, is muddled. This is so partly because he chose to suppress the price of capital assets in his statement of his liquidity-preference function. Instead of explicitly introducing both the price of capital assets and the terms on money loans in his discussion of portfolios, he phrased his argument in terms of interest rates. Furthermore, in a key discussion of the determination of the relative price of different capital and financial assets, Keynes retrogressed from the cyclical perspective dominant in the rest of the book to an equilibrium-growth perspective. As a result of these flaws, the full power of his reasoning was obscured and lost to the interpretive work that followed.

In this chapter we will start with an overview of capitalist financial relations in terms of cash flows, take up the liquidity-preference function without suppressing capital-asset prices, and examine how asset valuation and the financing of positions are related.

CASH FLOWS AND THE DEMAND FOR MONEY

In a capitalist economy, one way every economic unit can be characterized is by its portfolio: the set of tangible and financial assets it owns, and the financial liabilities on which it owes. (Leases and rent contracts are financial liabilities and assets; just like bonds, they set up cash flows.) In principle, the owned assets are marketable and the unit can assume additional financial liabilities.

Each economic unit makes portfolio decisions. A portfolio decision has two interdependent facets. The first relates to what assets are to be held, controlled, or acquired; the second relates to how the position in these assets—i.e., their ownership or control—is to be financed. In the terminology that Keynes uses, both assets and liabilities are annuities: they set up cash receipts or expenditures over some fixed or variable future time period. In today's language, assets and liabilities set up a dated sequence of anticipated cash flows, i.e., cash receipts or cash payments.

Various assets and liabilities differ in the nature of the cash flows they set up. The cash flows for any asset or liability may be dated, demand, or contingent; they may be unconditional or may depend upon the functioning of the economy; they may be associated with owning or using an asset, or with the purchase or sale of an asset. The variety of cash payments in a modern capitalist economy is great. All the factor-payment types, wages, rents, interest, and profits, are cash flows. So are taxes and transfer payments, payments for final and intermediate output, and payments on financial instruments.

Cash flows also vary in their assuredness. The cash flows that a specialized chemical plant will generate for its owning firm, as it is operated, depend upon market-determined revenues and costs. These in turn depend upon how the firm does as an enterprise in its industry, how the industry does, and how well or poorly the economy functions.

Furthermore, in principle an asset such as a chemical plant can generate a cash flow from outright sale. The outright sale of an ongoing specialized chemical plant is perhaps rare, although, when transactions involving transfers of operating affiliates are taken into account, such uses of tangible assets to raise cash are not so rare that the contingency may be ignored in valuing assets. In the aftermath of the collapse of the 1960s conglomerate mania in the United States, many conglomerates raised cash or decreased their cash commitments by divesting themselves of subsidiaries. Furthermore, there are less extreme alternatives to the sales of assets. Cash can be raised by pledging or mortgaging owned but previously unencumbered capital assets and, in an economy whose complex financial structure encompasses conglomerate corporations and holding companies, cash can be raised by pledging or selling the common stock of an operating subsidiary.

The cash flows an owning unit may generate by sale or hypothecation of operating tangible assets—such as a chemical plant—are subject to a great deal of variability. At any time the amount of money that can be raised by such a transaction depends upon the views of other operators and potential operators of chemical plants and of bankers, commercial and investment, about the ability of the chemical plant to generate cash flows under this or an alternative management, within the anticipated economic environment. The well-being of an ordinary business firm depends not only on the behavior of the market for its output and the terms upon which it can hire inputs, but also on the behavior of financial markets; on the terms on which it can borrow, sell assets, or float shares.

In contrast to the conditional character of the cash flows that a chemical plant may generate by being sold or by being operated, the cash flows that a treasury debt—such as a treasury bill—will generate as its contract terms are satisfied are, in nominal terms, assured; it is known beyond a reasonable doubt that the commitment by the government as stated in the instrument will be honored. Furthermore, in an advanced capitalist economy all treasury debt, and short-term treasury bills in particular, have quite broad, deep, and resilient markets; that is, there are many owners, the trading volume is large, and the price of the instrument will bounce back from price changes due to any short-run excess of supply or demand on the markets. In a quick sale, an owner of a short-term treasury-debt instrument can raise in cash just about the face value. For longer-run treasury debt, even though the fulfillment of the terms of the contract is assured, there are speculative, or conjectural, elements which enter into the decision to own such debt. This is so because price-level changes can affect the purchasing power of the cash flows, and the market price of a longer-term instrument at any date will reflect the current market interest rates of appropriate maturity.

Cash—money itself—is a peculiar and special asset from the perspective of cash flows and a world with complex financial commitments. Unlike savings accounts and treasury debt, money is a financial asset that nowadays yields no net cash flows from being held. That money and other financial assets fixed in nominal terms may appreciate in real value when output prices fall is not relevant at this point in the argument. The only special value of money is that in the form in which it exists it can be used to make cash payments. If a payment needs to be made and the paying unit owns treasury bills, then, almost always, the treasury bills need to be sold so that the proceeds can then be used to make the required payment. Possession of money eliminates the need for this transaction: it is convenient to hold "assets in the same standard as that in which future liabilities may fall due" (*GT*, p. 237).

In a world with private debts denominated in money, money is a safe asset for meeting such commitments. Money always has a ready market, for those units with commitments to pay money must engage in activities designed to obtain money. Money is not an asset with an invariant value with respect to income, for the price level of current output can change. Furthermore, the value of money in terms of other assets, including real capital, is not invariant—the money price of real and financial assets can change. Money is of invariant value only with respect to money contracts and payment commitments denominated in money—regardless of whether these payment commitments are due to debts, taxes, or current transactions.

Once financial interrelations are admitted to be of vital importance as determinants of how an economy functions, money and the monetary system are the natural starting point for economic theory. The special significance of money in a capitalist economy does not follow from the fact that money is the means of payment. Money is a means of payment in a socialist economy, but money is not a key variable in the determination of output, employment, investment, and prices, because a socialist economy lacks the financial interrelations of a capitalist economy. Speculation about the value of productive assets is a characteristic of a capitalist and not a socialist economy. The relevant paradigm for the analysis of a capitalist economy is not a barter economy; the relevant paradigm is a system with a City or a Wall Street where asset holdings as well as current transactions are financed by debts.

It is only conditionally true that

the peculiar feature of a money economy is that some commodities (in the present context all but one) are denied a role as a potential or actual means of payment. To state the same idea as an aphorism: *Money buys goods and goods buy money but goods do not buy goods.*[1]

This aphorism by Clower misses the distinguishing feature about the role of money in a capitalist economy. In a world with private financial liabilities which are used to acquire control or ownership of assets, these financial liabilities are what "buys" capital assets. The holder of a bank deposit is indirectly financing some position in capital assets.

These private financial liabilities set up cash-flow commitments. The cash to meet the liabilities of households and business firms will ordinarily flow from their income-producing operations, as wages, sales proceeds, or gross profits. The possession of money—and of financial assets that are near monies, i.e., savings accounts, certificates of deposits, etc.—acts as "insurance" against the economy, or particular markets, behaving in an inappropriate way; that is, in such a way that cash flows from operations or the ability to raise cash by financial transactions are insufficient to meet needs.

In addition, the economy contains financial units such as banks and insurance companies, whose normal functioning requires that they receive cash both as the terms of the financial contracts they own are fulfilled and from the sale, in well-behaved financial markets, of owned financial assets or of their own newly created liabilities. For such financial units, just as for households and firms, the possession of cash acts as insurance against shortfalls in cash receipts due to either default on contracts owned or a malfunctioning of the financial markets on which they sell assets or borrow.

MONEY-DEMAND OR LIQUIDITY-PREFERENCE EQUATIONS

In an economy with complex and sophisticated financial relations, the relevant set of transactions for determining the demand for money is far larger than the set of transactions in goods that are related

[1]Clower, "Foundations of Monetary Theory," pp. 207–8.

to final income, which the standard quantity theory emphasizes. Among the transactions that are relevant are the cash-payment commitments as stated in financial instruments and the purchase, sale, and financing of positions in assets. These additional uses of money in a world of uncertainty are the basis of Keynes's liquidity-preference doctrine.

The Fisher way of stating the fundamental quantity-theory equation of exchange, $MV = PT$ (M = money, V = velocity, P = price level, and T = transactions), where T encompasses all transactions that use or require money for payment, can capture the financial aspects of how money is used better than does the "Cambridge form" of the quantity theory equation, $M_D = kPO$. (M_D = money demand, k = proportion of income demanded in money, P = price level of final output, and O = real final output.) The Fisher form in its full extension, where $\Sigma M_i V_i = \Sigma P_j T_j$ (allowing for i different monies and velocities and j different price levels and transaction types), can draw attention to non-commodity transactions. The Fisher form in its income garb, $MV = PO$, and Cambridge form when written in the usual way, $M = kPO$, are limited to emphasizing the connection of the demand for money with the demand for final output. These output-related forms ignore the effect of financial transactions upon the demand for money.

In *The General Theory* Keynes distinguishes the transactions, precautionary, and speculative motives for holding money. His background leads him to begin from the Cambridge formulation, which is interpreted as emphasizing the motives for holding money. The transactions motive is "to bridge the interval between the receipt of income and its disbursement" (*GT*, p. 195), as well as "the interval between the time of incurring business costs and that of the receipt of the sale-proceeds" (*GT*, p. 195). When the precautionary motive is explained he emphasizes the importance of holding "an asset of which the value is fixed in terms of money to meet a subsequent liability fixed in terms of money" (*GT*, p. 196). When Keynes first discusses the speculative motive for holding money he describes it as being due to "the object of securing profit from knowing better than the market what the future will bring forth" (*GT*, p. 170). In *The General Theory* Keynes does not fully follow the lead of this definition of the speculative motive by emphasizing that securing profit by speculation involves the appreciation (or depreciation) of asset prices. The fundamental speculative demand for money centers around the extent to which borrowing takes place to finance positions in assets whose price may vary; these expected asset prices as well as the terms on money loans are the determinants of the speculative demand for money.

Keynes wrote the demand for money as

$$M = M_1 + M_2 = L_1(Y) + L_2(r) \quad [GT, \text{ p. } 199] \quad (1)$$

where L_1 is the liquidity function corresponding to an income Y "and L_2 is the liquidity function of the rate of interest r" (*GT*, pp. 199–200). In this formulation L_1 reflected the transactions motive and L_2 the speculative motive. Keynes here suppresses the expected price of capital assets as a determinant of the speculative demand for money. Our argument is that it is necessary to explicitly introduce the price level of capital assets, P_K, as a determinant of the demand for money so that changes in the quantity of money, which lead to a movement along a liquidity-preference function, or changes in uncertainty or in speculative expectations, which led to a shift in the liquidity-preference function, can affect the price of capital assets. Thus we should write

$$M = M_1 + M_2 = L_1(Y) + L_2(r, P_K) \quad (1')$$

where the rate of interest r is now restricted to the rate on money loans. In this formulation, if M is given, the speculative demand for money can act as a determinant of the price level of capital assets.

From Keynes's definition of the precautionary motive of the demand for money, in an economy where the amount of private debt outstanding can stand in varying relations with income, the demand for money should be written as

$$M = M_1 + M_2 + M_3 = L_1(Y) + L_2(r, P_K) + L_3(F) \quad (2)$$

where L_3 is the precautionary motive due to the outstanding private financial commitments, F. We can, if we wish, integrate the demand for finance, which Keynes acknowledged as relevant in his exchanges with Ohlin, into this formulation. Thus F would increase as planned or ex ante investment increased,[2] reflecting the precautionary demand for cash balances because future payment commitments increase owing to the increase in investment activity.

Furthermore, some financial instruments which we can call near

---

[2]Keynes, "Alternative Theories of the Rate of Interest," pp. 241–52, and Keynes, "The 'Ex-Ante' Theory of the Rate of Interest," pp. 663–69.

monies, *NM*, satisfy the insurance and precautionary demands for money. We therefore can hold that the net demand for money is

$$M = M_1 + M_2 + M_3 - M_4 = L_1(Y) + L_2(r, P_K) + L_3(F) - L_4(NM) \quad (3)$$

where L_4 is the liquidity effect of the near monies *NM*.

In equation 1 we have that for a given quantity of money, the higher income, the higher the interest rate. In equation 1' we have that for a given quantity of money, the higher income, the higher the interest rate, and the lower the price of capital—if the movement is along a liquidity-preference schedule. But if the higher income is interpreted as increasing the surety of income from capital-asset ownership, then the liquidity-preference function will shift, so that for a given quantity of money, the higher income, the higher the interest rate and the higher the price of capital assets.

In equation 2 we have that for a given quantity of money and a given level of income, the greater F, the amount of private financial commitments outstanding, the higher the rate of interest and the lower the price of capital assets. In equation 3 the greater the quantity of near monies—the greater the quantity of savings deposits and savings bonds —for a given quantity of money, income, and financial commitments, including the planned pace of investment, the lower the rate of interest and the higher the price of capital assets.

With the introduction of near monies we introduce, via the institutions whose liabilities are near monies, an endogenous determination of the effective quantity of money. Inasmuch as the creation of such near monies reflects a demand for financing, a period of financial innovation can lead to a rising price of capital assets side by side with rising interest rates on money loans. Therefore, the interest rate in a system in which banks and near banks determine the effective quantity of money can be regarded

as being determined by the interplay of the terms on which the public desires to become more or less liquid [borrow] and those on which the banking system is ready to become more or less unliquid [lend].[3]

In *The General Theory* the argument pointed toward, but did not fully explore, the multidimensional character of the demand for money. Being

---

[3]Keynes, "The 'Ex-Ante' Theory of the Rate of Interest," p. 666.

multidimensional, Keynes's argument could have been related to Fisher's transaction view of the demand for money. However, the truly novel feature in Keynes's formulation, which made it much more powerful than the cataloging of transaction types toward which Fisher pointed, is the tying of the speculative demand for money to interest rates and asset prices. It is unfortunate that in his statement of liquidity preference he uses the interest rate as both the term on money loans and as a proxy for the suppressed price level of capital assets, thus obscuring the argument.

THE VALUE OF ASSETS AND THE FINANCING OF POSITIONS

In the Viner rebuttal Keynes begins his discussion of the functions of money by noting that:

Money, it is well known, serves two principal purposes. By acting as a money of account it facilitates exchange without its being necessary that it should ever itself come into the picture as a substantive object. In this respect it is a convenience which is devoid of significance or real influence. In the second place, it is a store of wealth. So we are told, without a smile on the face. But in the world of the classical economy, what an insane use to which to put it! For it is a recognized characteristic of money as a store of wealth that it is barren; whereas practically every other form of storing wealth yields some interest or profit. *Why should anyone outside a lunatic asylum wish to use money as store of wealth?* [*QJE*, pp. 215–16; emphasis added]

The answer to Keynes's leading question is that the world we live in is not the world of "the classical economy"; the world is an uncertain world because there are yesterdays, todays, and tomorrows. Furthermore, this is a capitalist world in which units have portfolios—assets and liabilities which embody yesterday's views and both earn and commit today's and tomorrow's receipts. In a world with uncertainty, portfolios are of necessity speculative. The demand for money as a store of value exists because in a world where speculation cannot be avoided—where to decide is to place a bet—money is not barren. As has been pointed out earlier, money in our world has attributes of an insurance policy, in that possession of money protects against the repercussions of particular undesirable contingencies. Thus money is held because "The possession of actual money lulls our disquietude; and the premium which we require to make us part with money is the measure of the degree of our disquietude" (*QJE*, p. 216). Just as when insurance premiums rise, substitution against insurance will take place, so if the cost of holding money, interest rates, rises substitution against money will take place.

Keynes further notes that

The significance of this characteristic of money has usually been overlooked; and in so far as it has been noticed, the essential nature of the phenomenon has been misdescribed. For what has attracted attention has been the *quantity* of money which has been hoarded; and importance has been attached to this because it has been supposed to have a direct proportionate effect on the price-level through affecting the velocity of circulation. But the *quantity* of hoards can only be altered either if the total quantity of money is changed or if the quantity of current money-income (I speak broadly) is changed; whereas fluctuations in the degree of confidence are capable of having quite a different effect, namely, in modifying not the amount that is actually hoarded, but the amount of the premium which has to be offered to induce people not to hoard. And changes in the propensity to hoard, or in the state of liquidity-preference as I have called it, primarily affect, not prices, but the rate of interest; any effect on prices being produced by repercussion as an ultimate consequence of a change in the rate of interest. [*QJE*, p. 216]

But of course "an increased propensity to hoard raises the rate of interest and thereby lowers the price of capital assets other than cash."[4]

In his rebuttal to Viner Keynes explains that the speculative motive for holding money affects the price of capital assets by first affecting the rate of interest:

This, then, is the first repercussion of the rate of interest as fixed by the quantity of money and the propensity to hoard, namely, on the prices of capital-assets. This does not mean, of course, that the rate of interest is the only fluctuating influence on these prices. Opinions as to their prospective yield are themselves subject to sharp fluctuations, precisely for the reason already given, namely, the flimsiness of the basis of knowledge on which they depend. It is these opinions taken in conjunction with the rate of interest which fix their price. [*QJE*, p. 217]

In discussing the relation between the rate of interest and the price of capital assets Keynes was arguing in terms of two markets: one in which interest rates and money loans are determined, the other in which the prices of capital assets are determined. As phrased here, the relations are sequential in the sense that disequilibria, or changes, in one market affect another market, and each market has its own adjustment time.

It follows that the value of assets that yield cash flows depends upon

---

[4]Keynes, "Alternative Theories of the Rate of Interest," p. 251.

the premium that wealth owners are willing to pay for holding an insurance policy against uncertainty in the form of money. Money, for perhaps poorly considered reasons, is deemed to embody such insurance to a greater extent than other assets.

Once we acknowledge that money embodies an insurance policy, and that the relevant set of transactions for which money is used includes financial payments as well as payments that reflect the production process, then the question arises as to what is being insured against. Against what contingency is money being held?

One reason for holding money is that for an income recipient a "rainy day" may occur when cash flows due to income receipts unexpectedly decrease. However, liquid assets, such as savings deposits and bonds, if the assets are believed to be "safe," dominate money for this purpose. Another reason for holding money is that the possession of money helps avert the contingency that assets might have to be sold for cash under duress, i.e., that payments on liabilities may exceed available cash from operations or asset contracts. The possibility that assets may have to be sold to make payments due on liabilities raises the question of why the liability structure of an organization will be such that the cash-payment commitments cannot be satisfied by receipts from operations and the fulfillment of contractual terms on owned financial assets. What are the payments that may force asset sales?

Keynes dug deeper—but not clearly—into these problems in chapter 17 of *The General Theory*, "The Essential Properties of Interest and Money." In this chapter he discusses the valuation of assets. His discussion, though perceptive, is flawed because he does not explicitly introduce liability structures and the payment commitments they entail at this point, even though this entered into his definition of the precautionary demand for money. Furthermore chapter 17 is obscure because he slips, almost as if by second nature, back into the world of the classical economy. In chapter 17 the accumulation process that is described leads to a decline in the yields on reproducible assets—presumably because of diminishing productivity as factor proportions change. As a result, the implicit yield on money, because of its liquidity properties, will in time exceed the explicit yield available on newly produced assets. The old ideas, of which Keynes warned in his introduction, take over at least partially in chapter 17. At a crucial juncture in the argument, stagnationist and exhaustion-of-investment-opportunity ideas take over from a cyclical perspective in which investment, asset holdings, and liability structures are guided by speculative considerations.

In order to bring out the power of the ideas involved, we will undertake to adjust the argument of chapter 17 by explicitly considering liability structures and by setting the argument in a cyclical and speculative framework. As modified by these considerations, the argument of chapter 17 gives us the ingredients for an explanation of a speculative investment boom and of why such a boom contains, in the development of a crisis-prone setup, the seeds of its own destruction.

The succession of transitory states of the world that generates the cyclical time path of the economy depends upon the asset-valuation process hinted at, but not explained in a complete way, in chapter 17.

In this chapter Keynes reverted to a classical equilibrium growth and accumulation view of the economic process. The cycle encompassing booms and crises, so evident throughout the rest of *The General Theory* and the focus of his rebuttal to Viner, is missing through most of this chapter.

The vision of chapter 17 is that the marginal efficiency or yield of real assets is lowered as accumulation takes place, so that, ultimately, the marginal efficiency of every type of produced means of production falls below the implicit yield—marginal efficiency—that money earns in the form of liquidity. As accumulation takes place the anticipated yield on each type of produced real asset is forced, in some sequence, below the current return in kind that money yields. As the return in the form of quasi-rents on a particular asset falls below the threshold set by the implicit return on money, the production of this asset, i.e., investment, comes to a halt. Keynes argues that money rules the roost as the expected yield on real assets declines, because if the money rate of return on produced assets is to equal the implicit rate of interest on money, the quasi-rents will have to be supplemented by expected capital appreciation. That is, the current price of produced assets must fall so low (the anticipated appreciation in price must be so large) that the current price is below the anticipated cost of production of these assets.

A cyclical perspective combined with an explicit consideration of money flows yields a much more natural way of obtaining a current market price of produced assets lower than sticky production costs than that advanced by Keynes in chapter 17. Furthermore, this alternative way of generating the result is more consistent with the views of the capitalist process that permeate both *The General Theory* and the rebuttal to Viner.

The subject matter of chapter 17 is the relative price of assets, in particular items in the stock of capital assets. Keynes distinguishes "three attributes which different types of assets possess in different degrees": "Some assets produce a yield or output, q"; "Most assets except money suffer some wastage, or involve some cost through the mere passage of time . . . they involve a carrying cost, c"; and "Finally the power of disposal over an asset during a period may offer a potential convenience of security. . . . The amount . . . [in foregone cash flows] which they are willing to pay for the potential convenience or security given by this power of disposal (exclusive of yield or carrying cost attaching to the asset) we shall call its liquidity-premium, l" (*GT*, pp. 225–26).

Thus

the total return expected from the ownership of an asset over a period is equal to its yield minus its carrying cost plus its liquidity premium, i.e. to $q - c + l$. . . . The total return to different assets are made up in different degrees of these various specialized returns: For "instrumental capital" and "consumption capital". . . its yield should normally exceed its carrying costs, whilst its liquidity premium is probably negligible; [*GT*, p. 226]

whereas for money "its yield is *nil*, its carrying cost negligible, but its liquidity premium substantial" (*GT*, p. 226). It follows that

an essential difference between money and all (or most) other assets [is] that in the case of money its liquidity-premium much exceeds its carrying cost, whereas in the case of other assets their carrying costs much exceed their liquidity-premium. [*GT*, p. 227]

The explicit and implicit cash flow, $q - c + l$, is capitalized to yield a value of the asset which is the demand price. Keynes holds that "in equilibrium the demand prices . . . in terms of money will be such that there is nothing to choose in the way of advantage between the alternatives" (*GT*, pp. 227–28). Inasmuch as l is an income in kind and $q - c$ is a money flow, it is a combination of explicit and implicit cash flows that is capitalized at a common rate to yield the demand price for q yielding capital assets. However, the ratio of q to the demand price will vary inversely with the implicit yield l of the asset. If an asset is liquid the cash flow in the form of interest and profits per dollar of market value will be smaller than if the asset is illiquid. The visible rate of return on an asset will vary inversely with the quality of the market for the asset, or with the time to maturity, or with other measures of the ease of disposal and the certainty of its sale price.

Note that a value obtained by capitalizing q for an illiquid asset—one for which l is zero—is *not* a price for which the asset can be sold in the market; it is a pure valuation of expected cash flows from operations. For if it were a potential market price it would be at least a somewhat liquid asset, and the l factor would need to be considered as a determinant of its market value.

We have to look further into these cash flows; the cash flows an asset yields to its owner and the cash flow from "the power of disposal over an asset" (*GT*, p. 226) that Keynes makes much of. In particular we have to examine how the relative market prices of assets will vary as the value placed upon liquidity l varies.

Disposing of an asset by sale yields a cash flow toward the selling unit; that is, by selling assets a unit can generate a cash flow in its favor. This cash flow may be a multiple, substantially greater than 1, of the q's that an asset is expected to generate. How large this multiple is depends upon the capitalization rate and the expected duration of the cash flows. If there is an active market for an owned asset, then the power of disposal implies that a unit can by sale set off a cash flow in its favor at its owner's will. This offers

a potential convenience or security, which is not equal for assets of different kinds, though the assets themselves are of equal initial value. . . . The amount (measured in terms of itself) . . . which they are willing to pay for the convenience or security given by this power of disposal (exclusive of yield or carrying cost attached to the asset) we shall call its liquidity-premium "l." [*GT*, p. 226]

Note that in the above quotation the liquidity premium is not a differential in the price of the asset; rather it is a difference in the anticipated or contractual cash flows of different assets with the same market valuations.

Keynes distinguishes three types of assets: instrumental capital, a stock of liquid goods, and money. The instrumental capital produces a yield, q, the stock of liquid goods suffer some wastage or carrying costs, c, and money produces neither a yield nor imposes carrying costs, but is liquid, l—that is, it can readily be disposed of. The return q from an asset is the cash flow that the asset will yield from operations, or by contract. For real physical capital collected into production units by firms, q is the Marshallian quasi-rent—it is total revenue minus total out-of-pocket costs. Depreciation is an accounting allocation of a portion of the quasi-rent; it remains part of the relevant disposable cash flow. To Keynes the supply price of output was greater than the marginal out-of-pocket costs, even for a firm in a competitive industry, because of the need to add user costs to out-of-pocket costs (user costs are defined as the present value of the maximum expected quasi-rent foregone by using capital equipment today so that it is not available for use at a future date).

The nature of quasi-rents can be illustrated by referring to the cost curves of standard price theory. Diagram 4.1 is a standard set of short-run cost curves based upon the out-of-pocket costs for a firm in a competitive industry. The infinitely elastic demand curve confronting such a firm is given by *C-C'-C''*; the firm can sell any quantity it chooses at a price *OC*. The average variable cost curve (*AVC*) is total out-of-pocket (labor and material) costs for each output divided by output. In this exposition fixed or overhead labor and services are ignored. In drawing the *AVC* we make no allowance for capital consumption or what Keynes called user cost. User cost is not properly a cost; it really determines the minimum quasi-rent for each output that would induce the firm to use capital assets rather than leaving them idle.

Profit-maximizing output of the firm is *OO'*. The difference between

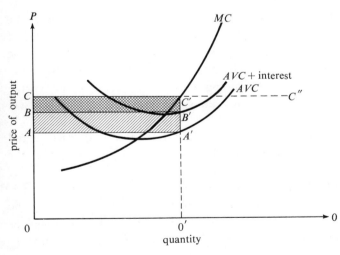

Diagram 4.1   COST CURVES

total receipts and total variable cost is the quasi-rent. In diagram 4.1, $OC \times OO'$ is the total revenue and $OA \times OO'$ is the total variable costs. The shaded area $ACC'A'$ is the quasi-rent, Keynes's q. If this firm has a debt structure, then over the period covered by the diagram, cash interest payments will be required. The interest payments are presumably independent of output; thus AVC plus interest is derived by adding total interest charges to the total variable costs. The area $ABB'A'$ represents the interest payments—in our interpretation, the c of Keynes. The difference between the gross quasi-rents and the interest payment is the gross profits before taxes.

If the debt contract provides for a sinking fund or includes some amortization of the principal of the debt, then the cash-payment requirements will be greater than the pure interest charge $ABB'A'$. Such financial considerations force the firm to use some of its gross profits before taxes to meet financial commitments. In fact if the financial contracts are sufficiently short, then the cash payments on financial contracts can exceed the total quasi-rents. The implications of this possible situation for the firm and for financial markets will be considered in what follows.

Thus q, the quasi-rent, is a cash flow that is independent of the liability structure of the producing unit. This is the concept of income used in determining the market value of the underlying physical assets. Presumably, in a perfect capital market, where uncertainty and liquidity do not affect the valuation of assets, $q - c$ capitalized would equal the market value of equities, c capitalized would equal the market value of debts, and the sum of the two would be invariant and equal to the capitalized value of q; that is, debt structure would not affect the valuation of a firm. For purposes of valuing liquidity in a cyclical context, the cash-flow concept for a firm must allow for financing charges and tax liabilities.

Keynes recognized that the stock of liquid goods entails wastage and carrying costs. He uses wheat as his example—fully realizing that the expected appreciation of wheat prices, which is necessary if it is to be profitable to hold wheat, must be large enough to compensate for wastage, storage-facility rental, and interest on the cost of the wheat over the period wheat is carried. Certainly if one thinks of carrying stocks such as wheat, one thinks of the financing charges. But this is *not* explicitly mentioned in chapter 17, although the money rate of interest is used in the example (*GT*, p. 233) in which Keynes determines the wheat rate of interest.

Consider a pure instrumental capital, yielding a quasi-rent, q, and a pure stock of liquid goods, the ownership of which entails a carrying cost, c. For liquid-stock items, the current demand price must be sufficiently below the expected market price at the end of the carrying period so that the expected capital appreciation will more than offset the financing costs and the wastage. The important thing to notice is that it is the current price of the wasting asset which adjusts so that all the current supply is either used or taken into stocks. If at an initial current price there is an excess supply, then prices will fall until either current use or additions to stocks absorb the excess supply. Simultaneously, it is current and anticipated prices which act as guides to production. If the carrying charges are high because of a floor to interest rates, owing to liquidity factors, then the current output of such goods will be affected by the current, depressed price of the stock.

Similarly for instrumental capital, if q decreases as capital is accumulated, then the price of such capital must fall, so that the rate of return equals the implicit liquidity rate on money.

For both liquid stocks and instrumental capital Keynes in chapter 17 sketches an accumulation process that staggers to a slowdown and ultimately halts. But the booms Keynes writes of in chapter 17, and in his rebuttal to Viner, end with the bang of a crisis and not the whimper of a stagnation. Keynes calls c carrying costs and notes that "in what follows we shall be exclusively concerned with $q - c$" (*GT*, p. 226). Extending Keynes, $q - c$ is the quasi-rents minus the carrying costs. For a set of assets collected in a firm, c is most importantly the cash flow set up by the liability structure.

Short liabilities and the liquidity they and stock-market assets presumably give the holder were targets, in the aftermath of the Great Depression, of critics of the institutional structure of the economy. To Professor Simons of Chicago, the flaw in the capitalist system centered around the short liabilities, in the form of demand deposits, that banks and other financial institutions put out. If in fact such deposits are withdrawn, then the cash a unit (e.g. a bank) is committed to pay can exceed the sum of the cash flow receipts and whatever initial cash the unit holds. An organization with a large volume of short liabilities is either implicitly or explicitly refinancing its position—placing debt to acquire the cash to pay debt—every time a short debt falls due.

A commercial bank is an example of an organization with debt that is short term relative to the assets owned. A demand deposit is a demand debt. Each time a check is drawn on a bank, a cash drain is set up. The bank assets generate cash by following a schedule given by the contracts. As its due date approaches a note owned by a bank generates cash flowing to the bank.

However, on any given day the cash flow from deposit withdrawals at a bank can far exceed the cash gain from contract fulfillments. If the banking system is functioning normally, there will be cash flows due to deposit additions at various banks that may very well completely offset the deposit withdrawals. If a bank has a net deficit, then the bank sells some so-called secondary reserve assets in the money market for cash, or it borrows cash by putting forth its own debt. In principle, resources to acquire these assets or debts exist in the banking system, for the net deficit of the particular bank must, by arithmetic, be offset by net surpluses someplace else in the system. (Because in fact different banks and different types of deposits have different reserve ratios, the deficits and surpluses might not be fully offsetting.)

Whenever a run on a bank or other organization takes place, and runs are not merely matters of history (the runoff of bank negotiable certificates of deposit in the United States during the credit crunch of 1966 and the 1970 runoff of commercial paper are examples of recent runs), the cash needed by some banks, financial institutions, or non-financial organizations to meet withdrawals exceeds the cash accretions at other banks or financial organizations from deposits or their equivalent. In these circumstances, the unit losing liabilities either becomes a forced seller of assets, becomes a necessitous borrower from other units at penalty terms, or fails because it is unable to meet its commitments. Corporations and households can be considered banks, in that they have cash flows to meet and sources of cash from operations (their participation in income production), financial assets, borrowings, and the sale of assets.

The fundamental speculative decision of a capitalist economy centers around how much, of the anticipated cash flow from normal operations, a firm, household, or financial institution pledges for the payment of interest and principal on liabilities. Liabilities (debts) are issued to finance—or pay for—positions in owned assets; for operating firms the plant and equipment are the owned assets. The liabilities set up dated, demand, and contingent cash-payment commitments. Each firm speculates when it undertakes such commitments. As it undertakes these commitments the firm envisages situations in which the payments can be met, as well as others in which they cannot be met or can be met only at a substantial cost. The firm in accepting a liability structure in order to hold assets is betting that the ruling situation at the future dates will be such that the cash payment commitments can be met: it is estimating that the odds in an uncertain future are favorable. Even though the contract may have additional protection to the lender embodied in other contract clauses, the unit acquiring the liability is also speculating, along with the firm, that these cash-flow commitments will be met. In a layered financial structure, the unit acquiring a liability may have liabilities of its own, and its ability to fulfill its obligations depends upon the cash flow it receives from its assets, i.e., other units' liabilities.

However, it is possible that a firm will have cash-payment commitments over a period which exceed its expected cash receipts from operations. A unit while investing in plant and equipment might well be in such a position. As the cash payments need to be made, the unit can sell financial assets, draw down cash, or sell its own debt.

In addition, a unit may have the principal amount of some debt outstanding falling due and not have the cash or liquid assets on hand to meet the payment. In these circumstances the firm may pay its due amount by issuing new debt; rolling over, or refunding, its debt. This is the common course for governments that have short-term debt such as treasury bills outstanding. It also is the normal course for consumer credit corporations which finance a portion of their position with short-term commercial paper and bank loans. Furthermore, nonfinancial firms will very often pay debt to a bank by loan renewals, or, if they borrow from many banks, a common practice in the United States, a firm may pay its debt to bank A by borrowing from bank B, etc.

How do units get into a position where their cash outflow due to commitments is greater than their cash inflow due to operations? One way is deliberate, when a unit is engaged in an investment program that requires external financing. Another way is by error, such as overestimating the net cash inflow, or by being unduly optimistic about sales or costs. A further way is by having debtors on owned contracts default —which in a closely articulated set of layered financial relations can have a domino effect. Firms may also deliberately and actively speculate by taking a chance that refinancing will be available at a reasonable rate. This will be done if more favorable financing terms are available on short-term liabilities than are available on long-term liabilities, or if terms on long-term liabilities are viewed as being unduly high, so that they are expected to be lower in the relevant future.

In order to acquire assets with a market value in excess of a unit's own net worth it is necessary to emit debt. One way to finance such positions is to emit debt which carries cash-flow commitments that are synchronized with the expected cash receipts, or quasi-rents. A strong-risk averter will engage in this type of hedge financing. However, there are potential financing organizations which value liquidity highly, and thus offer more satisfactory terms on instruments for which the repayment of principal leads to cash flows that exceed the cash flows anticipated from owned assets. Such a lending unit may value highly the cash flow due to the repayment of principal; it wants the liquidity due to owning short-term assets as well as the ability to redirect its resources without running any "market" risks. A borrowing unit therefore will have to balance the expected saving on financial costs due to lower financing rates against the hazard that the required cash may be available only at penal rates or terms when refinancing is necessary.

Thus each firm has a balance sheet, a collection of assets and liabilities, which yields a cash flow, q, from operations and contract fulfillment and which entails a cash flow, c, owing to the liabilities the firm has outstanding. There is a subset of assets in the balance sheet which have a good secondary market, so that the firm can expect to dispose of them at a fairly firm price. Furthermore, these assets can be disposed of without seriously affecting the q from plant and equipment. An operating firm therefore has to speculate on $q - c$, and on the assets to be owned which are valued for their disposal properties, i.e., assets which yield implicit returns in the form of l. A firm can acquire additional assets, which yield q, by increasing its liabilities, thus raising c, and by decreasing its liquid assets, thus lowering l. It can also increase its l by increasing its c; firms and households often have debts and own liquid assets.

This portfolio decision is a decision under uncertainty of the kind that Keynes discussed so eloquently in his rebuttal to Viner. The returns q are the returns to enterprise. The proportion of the returns committed by liabilities c and the proportion of assets owned that yield a return in the form of liquidity l are due to speculative decisions. Investment is the production allocation which increases the q yielding assets in an economy; the investing firm acquires these assets by putting out its liabilities, which increases the c it is committed to pay, or by decreasing its l assets. A decision to invest is a decision to emit liabilities or decrease liquidity: the cash received in exchange for commitments c is the currency used to pay for the investment.

Similarly, a decision to acquire second-hand capital goods—and to acquire control over other corporations—is a decision to emit liabilities that are obligations to make payments c or to decrease liquidity. In the corporate maneuverings, takeovers, mergers, and conglomerate expansions that characterize a boom, the c flow commitments increase relative to the expected q flow receipts. Furthermore, in the euphoric atmosphere of a boom, when optimistic views of the future prevail, the ratio of the market price of assets that command a liquidity premium l to the market price of other financial assets that yield c is decreased: liquid-asset interest rates rise relative to other rates.

Thus the fundamental speculation of a capitalist society has two facets: the acquisition of capital assets and the putting out of commitments to pay cash embodied in the liabilities used to finance such capital acquisitions. If the speculation is successful, then the cash flows, including appreciation of capital-asset prices resulting from the asset acquisition, will be more than sufficient to meet the payment commitments due to the liabilities. This will increase the capital value of the owning firm; that is, the market valuation of $q - c + l$ will increase by more than the cost of the investment.

In a world with a stock market, such successful speculation by firms results in an appreciation of the value of the stock of the firm. In a modern capitalist economy, the well-being of a firm's decision-makers is tied up through ownership, stock warrants, or bonuses in the firm's common stock doing well. Thus successful speculation in the acquisition of real assets—which increases q and makes q more secure—is an objective of business management. Businessmen, as they play the mixed game

of skill and chance that is business, are inescapably speculators. However, as Keynes remarked:

> Speculators may do no harm as bubbles on a steady stream of enterprise. But
> the position is serious when enterprise becomes the bubble on a whirlpool of
> speculation. When the capital development of a country becomes a by-product of
> the activities of a casino, the job is likely to be ill-done. [*GT*, p. 159]

With the stock market boom that accompanies an investment boom
there is a reciprocating stimulus—a positive feedback—between speculation on the exchanges and speculation by firms. A rise in the market
price of the common stock of a firm on the exchanges means that the
market valuation of the firm has increased—decreasing the ratio of cash-
payment commitments, c, to the market valuation of the firm. To bankers and other financers, such increased market valuation implies that the
firm can issue more debt—undertake additional commitments to pay
cash c. Furthermore, common shares, either by new public issues or by
direct payment, are often the currency used to acquire capital assets or to
take over firms. This means that during a stock market boom, the price
of capital assets and investment output may have fallen in the currency
used in their purchase, even though their money price may have risen.

An increase in the quantity of money relative to other assets and to the
cash-payment commitments, c, decreases the liquidity premium on
money, and thus the value of the liquidity embodied in different degrees
in other assets and debts. This will tend to increase the money price of
both debts which yield c and of capital assets which yield q, and it will
increase the price of capital assets and debts which embody relatively
little l as compared to those assets and debts which owe a great deal of
their market value to their liquidity. If we write P_K for the capitalized
value of the q's an asset is expected to yield, we have that

$$P_K = K(q,M)$$

where P_K is the price of an existing capital asset and M is the money
supply. We also have that

$$\frac{dP_K}{dq} > 0 \quad \text{and} \quad \frac{dP_K}{dM} > 0.$$

We expect that the power of money to raise the price of capital assets is limited, so that there exists a maximum

$$\hat{P}_K \underset{M \to \infty}{=} K(M,q).$$

This impact of the supply of the secure asset M upon the price of capital assets can be combined with the speculative pricing of K, which reflects the desired, or acceptable, liability structure, i.e., the willingness to purchase capital assets by issuing debts which commit future payments, c, such debts being a "money" that is specialized to the purchase of capital assets. Given an existing liability structure embodying payment commitments, c, and the expected cash flows, q, the greater the acceptable cash-payment commitments, $\hat{c}$, relative to expected cash flows, q, the higher the price of capital assets in terms of money. Thus we have

$$P_K = K(M, q, \hat{c} - c) \qquad \text{where} \qquad \frac{dP_K}{d\hat{c}} > 0.$$

The acceptable $\hat{c}$ given q is a shift parameter in the valuation relation; $\hat{c}$ reflects speculative elements in the financing of positions in the stock of capital assets, in that it embodies views as to the likelihood that "operations" will generate sufficient cash to meet the payments on debts and that financial markets will function well. Inasmuch as P_K (the price of a unit in the stock of capital assets) is a determinant of the demand price for a unit of newly produced capital assets, i.e., investment, variations in P_K become a proximate cause of variations in investment; variations in P_K will occur as M changes with a stable function and as the function shifts. The function will shift as the subjective views about prospective yields, the q's, and the value of liquidity, l, change. Because both the prospective yields and the premiums on liquidity reflect views about the future, both the views held and the confidence with which they are held are subject to "sudden and violent changes" of the kind Keynes wrote about. Thus the P_K function, though a useful expository tool, shifts around, rising during boom times and collapsing after a crisis.

In the argument that follows we will use the P_K function to replace the standard liquidity-preference function. It is preferable to the liquidity-preference function because it quite clearly generates prices for items in

the stock of capital assets and financial assets; it also is preferable because, as it has been derived, the P_K function includes in the valuation of
assets their ability to generate cash by sale—i.e., their liquidity. Inasmuch as the premium which units will pay for this ability to generate
cash will vary, the ability of monetary changes to affect the economy
becomes dependent upon what is happening to liquidity premiums.

The above analysis leads us both to the relative prices of different
assets and to the general price level of capital assets. The prices of capital
assets, which yield q's and l's, and debts, which yield c's and l's, in
different proportions are related to the supply of money, which only
yields an income in kind l and which, by definition, has a price of 1. The
prices that are generated are the prices of the units in the stock of assets,
both capital assets and financial assets. However, capital assets can be
produced, and new debt contracts can be written. We now have to
investigate the relation between the price of capital assets and their production, i.e., investment.

Note that in the background to this discussion the wage rate and the
price level of output have, implicitly, remained constant. The model is a
two-price-level model, where, in the short run, current output and
capital-asset prices depend upon different market processes. Whereas
wages and the current costs of producing output, and thus the offer
prices of current output, move sluggishly, the prices of units in the stock
of capital assets and, more directly, the price of equity shares traded on
the exchanges can move rapidly. Thus the relation between the two
price levels can change quite quickly; we have a price level of current
output which is in principle sluggish, and a price level of capital assets
which is in principle volatile.

‹5›

The Theory
of Investment

INTRODUCTION

Keynes characterized his contribution as "a theory of why output and employment are so liable to fluctuation" (*QJE*, p. 221). In the "pure" theory, where government and foreign demand are ignored, employment depends upon consumption and investment demand. Consumption demand is passive, as it "depends mainly on the level of income" (*QJE*, p. 219), that is, on the sum of consumption and investment demand.

Keynes's theory is one in which investment is the active, driving force causing that which must be explained, fluctuations:

The theory can be summed up by saying that, given the psychology of the public, the level of output and employment as a whole depends on the amount of investment. I put it in this way, not because that is the only factor on which aggregate output depends, but because it is usual in a complex system to regard as the *causa causans* that factor which is most prone to sudden and wide fluctuations. More comprehensively, aggregate output depends on the propensity to hoard, on the policy of the monetary authority as it effects the quantity of money, on the state of confidence concerning the prospective yield of capital-assets, on the propensity to spend and on the social factors which influence the level of money-wage. But of these several factors *it is those which determine the rate of investment which are most unreliable, since it is they which are influenced by our views of the future about which we know so little.* [*QJE*, p. 221; emphasis added]

Thus the core of *The General Theory* is the theory of investment and why it is so prone to fluctuate. The glib assumption made by Professor Hicks in his exposition of Keynes's contribution that there is a simple, negatively sloped function, reflecting the productivity of increments to the stock of capital, that relates investment to the interest rate is a caricature of Keynes's theory of investment. The problem in this chapter is to formulate with precision Keynes's theory of investment, which relates the pace of investment not only to prospective yields but also to ongoing financial behavior.

INVESTMENT AND INTEREST

Keynes's theory of investment links the fluctuating pace of investment, which is an output (real sector) concept, to variables which are determined in financial markets. The focus for financial markets is on the rate of interest. "Interest on money means precisely what the books on arithmetic say that it means; that is to say it is simply the premium obtainable on current cash over deferred cash. . . ."[1] That is, the rate of interest always refers to financial contracts such as bonds, mortgages, bank debts, deposits, etc.: current cash is the amount of the loan, deferred cash is the set of interest and principal repayments as stated in the contract. If P_L is the amount of the loan (current cash) and if the contract calls for a set of payments C_i, then the rate of interest is the arithmetic discount factor which equates the two.

There are two basic types of information which output-producing —the real sector—feeds into the determination of investment. One is the prospective yield:

When a man buys an investment or a capital-asset, he purchases the right to a series of prospective returns, which he expects to obtain from selling its output, after deducting the running expenses of obtaining this output, during the life of the asset. The series of annuities Q_1, Q_2, . . . Q_n it is convenient to call the *prospective yield* of the investment. [*GT*, p. 135; Keynes's emphasis.]

Note that when Keynes writes of investment or a capital asset to be

[1]Keynes, "The Theory of the Rate of Interest," p. 418.

used in production he uses upper-case Q's to refer to the prospective yields, and when he refers to the holding of capital assets in portfolios, the yields, as in the previous chapter, are written with lower-case q's. Both the Q's and the q's clearly are cash flows.

The prospective returns from the ownership of a capital asset are compounded from two items: the cost relations, which reflect the known production relations, and estimates as to how the economy and the producing unit will do. Thus the Q's embody present views about the future, and therefore are prone to change as views about the future change.

The second output-producing determinant of investment is the supply price of investment output:

> Over against the prospective yield of the investment we have the *supply price* of the capital-assets, meaning by this, not the market price at which an asset of the type in question can actually be purchased in the market, but the price which would just induce a manufacturer to newly produce an additional unit of such assets, i.e. what is sometimes called its *replacement* cost. [*GT*, p. 135; Keynes's emphasis.]

The supply price of the capital asset can best be interpreted as a schedule, in which higher demand prices for capital assets will yield greater outputs of investment goods. This schedule is assumed stable in the relevant time period. In the relevant short run, substantial shifts of this schedule will take place only if the wage rate changes; if the analysis is carried on in wage units, in the short run significant changes will not take place. (Changes in user costs can cause changes in the supply price; at present we are ignoring this complication.) In the longer run this supply curve will shift with changes in productivity, but in a cyclical perspective this longer run need not concern us.

The two stable functions in Keynesian theory are the supply schedule for capital assets and the consumption function, when both are measured in wage units. In nominal terms these functions shift whenever the wage rate changes. The other functions, which directly embody present views about the future, are not stable, i.e., they are prone to shift.

Since investment fluctuates, and since one of the basic ingredients in the analysis of investment—the supply schedule of investment goods—is a stable function, the observed fluctuations must be due to variations in (1) some combination of the prospective yields, as determined by both the production of income and views about the future; (2) the interest rate as determined in financial markets, or (3) the linkage between the capitalization factor for prospective yields on real-capital assets and the interest rate on money loans. The linkage reflects the uncertainty felt by entrepreneurs, households, and bankers. In fact, Keynes uses all three of these to explain the fluctuations of investment.

The prospective yields—the Q's—are quasi-rents, they are not measures of the marginal productivity of capital. To Keynes, thinking within a cyclical framework, the marginal productivity of capital was an ambiguous concept. The Q's are the result of the scarcity of capital:

> It is much preferable to speak of capital as having a yield over the course of its life in excess of its original cost, than as being *productive* [Keynes's emphasis]. For the only reason why an asset offers a prospect of yielding during its life services having an aggregate value greater than its initial supply price is because it is *scarce* [Keynes's emphasis]. . . . If capital becomes less scarce, the excess yield will diminish, without its having become less productive—at least in the physical sense. [*GT*, p. 213]

Furthermore, the Q's are *not* the marginal productivities that enter into distribution theory:

> The ordinary theory of distribution, where it is assumed that capital is getting *now* its marginal productivity (in some sense or other), is only valid in a stationary state. The aggregate current return to capital has no direct relationship to its marginal efficiency. . . . [*GT*, p. 139]

Whereas the productivity of a capital asset in conventional theory is technologically determined, the current scarcity yield of a capital asset depends upon the varying fortunes of industries, locations, and business conditions. In fact, over a business cycle the "scarcity" of capital varies. Depressions are characterized by idle men and machines, booms by shortages of both labor and capital assets.

The cash flows that capital assets are expected to generate as they are used in production and the supply schedule for newly produced capital assets (i.e., investment goods) are the foundation stones on which Keynes builds the real-sector influences upon investment. The cash flows are obviously a flow over a time period, whereas the supply price is a current value. As they stand, these basic concepts are not commensurable. A problem that must be faced is to construct a connection between the two.

This is done in two ways in *The General Theory*. The way that has entered the standard models is to construct a negatively sloped relation between investment and a discount rate—called the marginal-efficiency-of-capital schedule. The other is to capitalize the Q_i's to generate a demand price for investment output. Keynes apparently believed that the two constructs are equivalent and seemed to attach no great importance to the different modes of exposition. He emphasized the negatively sloped schedule in *The General Theory* and the alternative demand price for investment output in his reply to Viner.

However, like many choices that, when made, apparently make no difference, this choice of construct has had unfortunate consequences. Before we argue that point, let us go through Keynes's derivation of the schedule of the marginal efficiency of capital and his almost casual statement of the alternative capitalizing approach.

Both the marginal-efficiency-of-capital approach and the capitalizing of Q_i involve a bit of arithmetic. For the derivation of the marginal efficiency of capital we have a supply schedule of investment which says that the supply price, P_I, equals a function, rising, of investment, I:

$$P_I = P_I(I). \tag{1}$$

In addition we have

$$P_I(I) = \frac{Q_1(K_1,Y_1)}{1 + r_1} + \frac{Q_2(K_2,Y_2)}{(1 + r_2)^2} + \cdots + \frac{Q_n(K_n,Y_n)}{(1 + r_n)n}. \tag{2}$$

Equation 2 is the arithmetic formula that links prospective yields and the supply prices of investment. As P_I increases with unchanging Q's, the r's must decline to preserve the equality. If we assume that $r = r_1 = r_2 = r_3 = \ldots = r_n$, we have an nth degree polynomial in r, which in principle can be solved for one or more r's of the right order of magnitude. If we don't assume equal r's, then we have a complicated additional problem, which involves additional equations, of determining the term structure of interest rates. If the Q's are all equal and continue in perpetuity, then the simple capitalization formula applies:

$$P_I = \frac{Q}{r} \qquad \text{or} \quad r = \frac{Q}{P_I} \tag{3}$$

The r is dimensionally equal to the interest rate that appears, either explicitly or implicitly, in loan contracts.

In formulas 1 and 2 above the supply price of newly produced capital assets is explicitly written as a function of the pace of investment. We also have that

$$\frac{dP_{(I)}}{d(I)} > 0. \tag{4}$$

Furthermore, as the quasi-rents Q depend upon the scarcity of capital, then regardless of the cyclical state

$$\frac{\partial Q_i(K_i, Y_i)}{\partial (K_i)} < 0. \tag{5}$$

If we assume that the amount of capital, K_i, in future periods, $i > 1$, is positively related to the pace of investment in period 1, then in equation 2 the greater I, the greater P_I and the smaller the subsequent Q's. The r's that equate the current supply price of capital and the future prospective yields fall as the current pace of investment increases; r is called a discount rate. Keynes defined "the marginal efficiency of capital as being equal to that rate of discount which would make the present value of the series of annuities given by the returns expected from the capital-asset during its life just equal to its supply price" (GT, p. 135).

Keynes derives the negatively sloped relation between investment and the interest rate in the following basic passage:

If there is an increased investment in any given type of capital during any period of time, the marginal efficiency of that type of capital will diminish as the investment in it is increased, partly because the prospective yield will fall as the supply of that type of capital is increased and partly because, as a rule, pressure on the facilities for producing that type of capital will cause its supply price to increase. . . . Thus for each type of capital we can build up a schedule, showing by how much investment in it will have to increase within the period, in order that its marginal efficiency should fall to any figure. We can then aggregate these schedules for the different types of capital. . . . We shall call this the investment demand-schedule; or alternatively the schedule of the marginal efficiency of capital. [GT, p. 136]

Furthermore, "the rate of investment will be pushed to the point on the investment demand schedule where the marginal efficiency of capital in general is equal to the market rate of interest" (GT, p. 136–37).

Thus Keynes constructed a negatively sloped schedule, to use in linking the interest rate determined in financial markets to the pace of investment, by combining decreasing prospective yields with accumulation and a rising supply price of capital-goods output. He may have confused the influence of different stocks of capital assets with the influence of different rates of production of capital assets. This negatively sloped schedule led Keynes to the erroneous view: "Nor is there any material difference . . . between my schedule of the marginal efficiency of capital or investment demand-schedule and the demand curve for capital contemplated by some of the classical writers" (*GT*, p. 178). Furthermore, by identifying the discount rate derived in formulas 1 and 2 with the interest rate on financial assets, this misleading construct led Keynes to the readily misunderstood statement that "The creation of new wealth wholly depends on the prospective yield of the new wealth reaching the standard set by the current rate of interest" (*GT*, p. 212).

This choice of construct by Keynes led to an undue emphasis upon the interest rate, which to Keynes was always an attribute of money loans, as the tune caller and to too ready acceptance of the proposition that the marginal efficiency-of-capital schedule was not essentially different from the negatively sloped investment schedules that were drawn by classical economists.

Immediately after the passage cited above in which the marginal efficiency of capital schedule is derived (*GT*, p. 136) Keynes wrote:

> The same thing can also be expressed as follows. If Q_r is the prospective yield from an asset at time r, and d_r is the present value of £$_1$ deferred r years *at the current rate of interest*, $\Sigma Q_r d_r$ is the demand price of the investment; and investment will be carried to the point where $\Sigma Q_r d_r$ becomes equal to the supply price of the investment as defined above. If, on the other hand, $\Sigma Q_r d_r$ falls short of the supply price, there will be no current investment in the asset in question. [*GT*, p. 137]

Even though this statement is on the right track, it contains an ambiguity, for it is not clear if d_r represents the capitalization factor on all assets or on the specific asset that yields particular expected Q's. Nevertheless, it is an alternative construct for the determination of the demand for newly produced capital assets; it focuses upon capitalizing prospective yields. If correctly interpreted, it allows explicitly for two attenuating factors between productivity and investment, the first being variability in the prospective yields and the second variability in the relation between the present value, or capitalization rate, d_r in the above quotation, and the market rate of interest on money loans. The capitalizing formula is a more natural format for the introduction of uncertainty and risk preference of asset holders into the determination of investments than is the marginal efficiency schedule, which has been too casually linked by both Keynes and his interpreters to the productivity-based investment functions of the older, standard theory.

When Keynes undertook short expositions of the content of *The General Theory* after it appeared, he emphasized the price of capital assets. There is

a tendency for capital assets to exchange, in equilibrium, at values proportionate to their marginal efficiencies in terms of a common unit. That is to say, if r is the money rate of interest (i.e. r is the marginal efficiency of money in terms of itself) and y is the marginal efficiency of a capital asset A in terms of money, then A will exchange in terms of money at a price such as to make $y = r$.[2]

He continues by noting that:

If the demand price of our capital asset A thus determined is not less than its replacement costs, new investment in A will take place. . . . Thus the price system resulting from the relationship between the marginal efficiencies of different capital assets including money, measured in terms of a common unit, determines the aggregate rate of investment.[3]

In this passage Keynes says clearly that the demand price of a particular capital asset depends upon capitalization of its yields—our previous Q's. However, he is still tied to the standard interest-rate terminology. He first translates the yields into an internal rate of return presumably by attaching some price to the capital asset. It is the demand price, however, which he has to determine, and it is confusing to first assign a price to the capital asset to determine its yield in terms of money.

The capitalization of the prospective yields to generate a demand price for capital assets is a more natural way to approach the problems of fluctuating investment than the marginal-efficiency-of-capital schedule; a direct approach through the Q's and specific capitalization factors is more precise than an approach by way of relative marginal efficiencies. First of all, the Q's are not submerged, as in the alternative approach; second, the capitalization factor, which can have a varying ratio to the market rate of interest on secure loans because of the different values placed upon liquidity, is explicitly considered. Furthermore, two

[2]Ibid., p. 419.
[3]Ibid.

market-determined prices are dimensionally equivalent to the capitalized value of the Q's: the market price for items in the stock of capital assets and the price of equities, of shares.

Share prices affect the marginal efficiency of capital, as "a high quotation of existing equities involves an increase in the marginal efficiency of the corresponding type of capital" (*GT*, p. 151). More directly, share prices together with the market value of debts give us a market valuation of the bundles of capital assets collected in a firm. If the market valuation is high relative to the supply price of such assets newly produced, then presumably the pace of investment in such assets will be stepped up. Thus in the capitalization approach the market price of shares can be integrated into the analysis quite readily: the higher the market valuation of shares for a given interest rate and set of yields, the greater the capitalization factor on the prospective yields.

The fundamental relation in the theory of investment is the demand price of capital assets as determined by the capitalization of prospective yields. Let us assume that the prospective yields, the Q's, of a capital asset do not change during the diagramatic exercise below (diagram 5.1; this diagram is an expository device—the fundamental position of the argument that these yields fluctuate has not been adandoned).

With given prospective yields, the Q_i's, the demand price of a representative investment good is given by the price of the stock P_{K_i} of such capital assets. This can be written as $P_{K_i} = C_i(Q_i)$ when C_i is the

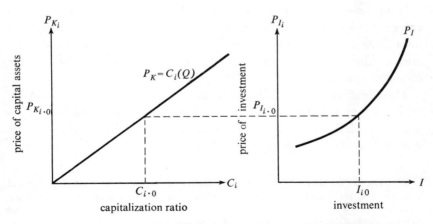

Diagram 5.1   PRICE OF CAPITAL ASSETS AND INVESTMENT

capitalization factor, what Keynes identified as "the present value of £1 deferred" (*GT*, p. 137). In diagram 5.1 the P_{K_i} function is a straight line in C_i; if $C_i = C_{io}$ then the price of this capital asset is $P_{K_{io}}$. In this case the capitalization factor is specific to the particular Q_i. If there is a perfect capital market, so that financial resources for investment are available without limit at terms that are independent of the amount taken, and if these terms are consistent with the capitalization rate C_{io}, then production of the investment good will be carried to the point where the supply price of the investment good, $P_{I_{io}}$ equals the demand price, $P_{K_{io}}$, that is, I_{io} of investment will be produced.

The query now is what determines the capitalization rate. For this part of our argument we shall assume that the rate of interest on money loans—the price of today's money in terms of deferred money—is given. We therefore know that if the prospective yields were contractual cash-payment commitments on money loans, then the price of that contract will be $P_l = C_l(CC)$, *where* C_l is the capitalization rate for money loans and CC is the contractual cash-payment commitment.[4]

The relation between C_i and C_l depends upon market evaluations of the security of owning rights to a certain or protected contractual cash commitment, CC, as against owning rights to a fluctuating, uncertain market yield, Q. The price of the instrument with contractual cash payments reflects both the surety due to the known cash flows on the debt and the liquidity due to the relative marketability of the debt as compared to a capital asset.

If we define a state of uncertainty as the appreciation that contingencies exist, together with an evaluation of the alternative outcomes, then, for a given state of uncertainty, we can write $C = \mu C_L$, the capitalization rate of capital assets is some ratio, $0 < \mu < 1$, of the capitalization rate on money loans.

Thus in diagram 5.2, if we substitute C_l for C_i along the x-axis between the money rate of interest and the price of capital assets, the price of capital assets relative to the price of debts is conditional on the state of uncertainty as given by μ. As μ changes, the P_K line will rotate:

---

[4]In chapter 4, we discussed the three attributes of assets, which we labeled q, the yield, c, the carrying costs, and l, the implicit liquidity yield. The capitalization rate for money loans is labeled C_l to indicate that the return on such assets does include some implicit liquidity yields—although if the only yield were liquidity, then the contractual cash payments would be one dollar per dollar of current price.

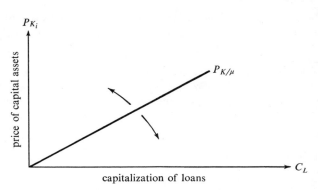

Diagram 5.2 *PRICE OF CAPITAL ASSETS*

an increase in μ, a decrease in the state of uncertainty, so to speak, will rotate the P_K line counterclockwise, increasing the price of capital assets relative to the price of debts. Another way of phrasing this would be to say that the value of both debts and capital assets depends upon the value being placed upon the liquidity of an asset, the implicit cash flows, l, that were discussed earlier. If capital assets embody less liquidity than debts, and if the value of liquidity decreases, then the price of capital assets will rise relative to both money and debts.

If we look at the determination of the rate of interest on money loans, the position of Keynes is clear:

the current rate of interest depends . . . not on the strength of the desire to hold wealth but on the strengths of the desire to hold it in liquid and in illiquid forms respectively, *coupled with the amount of the supply of wealth in the one form relatively to the supply of it in the other* . . . [*GT*, p. 213; my emphasis added]

Thus the rate of interest on a fixed supply of money loans (outstanding contracts) will vary inversely with the money supply, and the capitalization rate will vary directly with the money supply.

Furthermore, Keynes holds that the effect of the money supply upon the rate of interest on money loans tapers off as the ratio of money loans to money decreases. In principle, the rate of interest on money loans can get so low that further increases in the money supply will not effectively lower the rate of interest on money loans:

after the rate of interest has fallen to a certain level, liquidity-preference may become virtually absolute in the sense that almost everyone prefers cash to holding a debt which yields so low a rate of interest. [*GT*, p. 207]

After some point, increasing the ratio of money to money loans will not appreciably lower the rate of interest on money loans. In addition, for practical business loans:

the rate of interest which the typical borrower has to pay may decline more slowly than the pure rate of interest, and may be incapable of being brought, by the methods of the existing banking and financial organization, below a certain minimum figure. [*GT*, p. 208]

Thus the capitalization rate C_l on money loans is a function of the money supply, $C_l = Q(M)$, such that

$$\frac{\partial [C_l]}{\partial M} > 0, \quad \text{and} \quad \left| \frac{C_l}{M \to \infty} \right. \text{ is some finite number.}$$

Thus with a given state of liquidity preference which determines C_l and a given differential between the capitalization rate applicable to a capital asset and that applicable to money loans, which also reflects the state of liquidity preference, a given prospective yield on a capital asset Q_i will be transformed into a function relating the demand price of this capital asset to the quantity of money. This function will be such that

$$\frac{\partial P_{K_i}}{\partial M} > 0, \quad \frac{\partial_2 P_K}{\partial M^2} < 0, \quad \text{and} \quad \frac{P_{K_i}}{M \to \infty} = \hat{P}_{K_i}.$$

That is, this demand price of assets will increase as the quantity of money increases, this demand price will increase at a decreasing rate as the money supply increases, and for any set of prospective Q's there is a finite maximum to the price of a capital asset that can be achieved by increasing the money supply.

Thus

$$P_{K_i} = P_{K_i}(M, Q_i)$$

for any particular capital asset. This function subsumes a relation between a pure rate of interest and the quantity of money and a particular differential between the capitalization rate implied by the pure rate of interest and the capitalization rate on the particular capital asset K_i. This differential reflects the state of uncertainty with regard to the expected Q_i's as well as the liquidity value assigned to the asset K_i. It is not too heroic to assume that these uncertainty and liquidity attributes of capital assets tend to remain in somewhat fixed relation among the various kinds of capital assets, or if the relation changes over a business cycle the changes are in a predictable relation one to another. Thus from the argument that the price of a particular capital asset depends upon the quasi-rents it will earn and the quantity of money, we can move to the proposition that the price level of capital assets depends upon the aggregate expected quasi-rents and the quantity of money. In diagram 5.3 we relate the price level of capital assets and the quantity of money in a manner that is consistent with the relation between the price of a capital asset and money.

The fundamental fact about this aggregate $P_K(M, Q)$ function is that it is unstable. "If . . . we are tempted to assert that money is the drink which stimulates the system to activity, we must remind ourselves that there may be several slips between the cup and lip" (*GT*, p. 172). From our argument, the slippage may come from: (1) the link between the quantity of money and the interest rate on money loans; (2) the link between the interest rate on money loans and the capitalization rate on particular streams of prospective yields; (3) fluctuations in prospective yield due to changes in longer-term expectations.

As a result of these slippages, there are situations in which money may well call the tune, in the sense that modest changes in the money supply will affect modest changes in investment and thus in aggregate demand; on the other hand, there are situations in which the influence of the

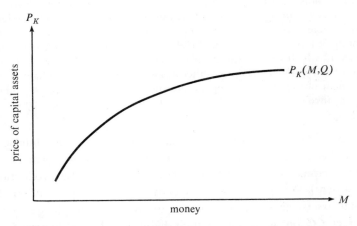

Diagram 5.3   PRICE OF CAPITAL ASSETS AND MONEY

money supply is much attenuated. Variations in the linkages as well as fluctuations in the prospective yield can well offset the influence of money.

Thus Keynes offered an explanation of why investment was not closely tied to production-function concepts and why the money supply was an erratic tune caller for investment. Although he hinted at the various states of the economy which succeed one another in an irregular sequence, and thus constitute the trade cycle, he never explicitly developed a theory of the boom and the crisis. This was so because, except for asides and hints, he never articulated a model—or an explanation—of how the liability structure of firms, banks, and other financial institutions evolve and how the endogenous generation of money and money substitutes takes place.

LIABILITY STRUCTURES AND THE PACE
OF A UNIT'S INVESTMENT

Although Keynes did not go into the details of how finance affected system behavior, he emphasized that in an economy with borrowing and lending, finance took on a special importance:

> Two types of risk affect the volume of investment which have not commonly been distinguished, but which it is important to distinguish. The first is the entrepreneur's or borrower's risk and arises out of doubts in his own mind as to the probability of his actually earning the prospective yield for which he hopes. If a man is venturing his own money, this is the only risk which is relevant.
>
> But where a system of borrowing and lending exists, by which I mean the granting of loans with a margin of real or personal security, a second type of risk is relevant which we may call the lender's risk. This may be due to either a moral hazard i.e. voluntary default or other means of escape, possibly lawful, from the fulfillment of the obligation, or the possible insufficiency of the margin of security i.e. involuntary default due to the disappointment of expectation. [GT, p. 144]

Loans, mortgages, bonds, and shares are the currency business firms use, either directly or indirectly after first exchanging them for money, to buy capital assets from the market, or from new production (i.e., investment). As against the prospective yield, Q, on additions to their capital assets, firms which finance in this manner pledge to pay, by contract CC on additions to their liabilities. Except when it involves shares this pledge is contractual, with penalties for default; for shares any deviation of dividends from the expected will affect equity prices.

Each acquisition of a capital asset, either from the market or from new production of capital assets, when financed in this way involves a margin of security. Typically, additional capital assets are acquired partially by own funds and partially by borrowed or outside funds, new-share capital being one class of outside funds. As was emphasized earlier, the fundamental speculative decision by a firm is how to finance control over its needed capital assets: how much by the firm's own resources and how much by borrowed resources. This decision is a determinant of both the firm's size, as measured by capital assets or sales, and the rate of growth of the firm's capital assets and sales.

Let us examine the financing behavior of a representative investing firm.

Such a firm expects this coming period's gross profits after taxes, and after its required payments on its debts and its dividends to stockholders, to be $\hat{Q}_i$; $\hat{Q}_i$ is independent of the level of the firm's own investment, although aggregate investment, by affecting income, affects the aggregate $\hat{Q}$. $\hat{Q}_i$ is the internal financing that the firm expects will be available this coming period.

We also assume that the supply price of the capital asset it expects to purchase, P_{I_1}, determined by the producers of capital assets, is independent of the amount purchased by this firm; the firm is not so large a buyer of capital assets that its own demand affects the price. Therefore, the amount of investment which can be financed internally is $\hat{I}_i = \hat{Q}_i/P_I$; that is, $P_{I_1}\hat{I}_i = \hat{Q}_i$; the internal financing constraint is a rectangular hyperbola in the (P_I, I) plane ($\hat{Q}_i \text{-} Q_i$ in diagram 5.4).

In diagram 5.4, if the firm would buy $\hat{I}$ of investment at P_I it could finance the entire amount internally. If the firm purchases $I_1 > I$ of investment at P_I, then $P_I I_1 - \hat{Q}$ will be debt financed: the firm will promise to pay future cash, in the form of various flows, CC, in exchange for $P_I I_1 - \hat{Q}$ of current cash. There is an exception. The firm may have excess current cash or marketable securities, which it uses to finance these purchases. There are valid reasons in a world of uncertainty why a firm or household with debts will also own idle money and other financial assets, i.e., other unit's debts. In part, this cash and financial-asset position insulates the normal operations of the firm from

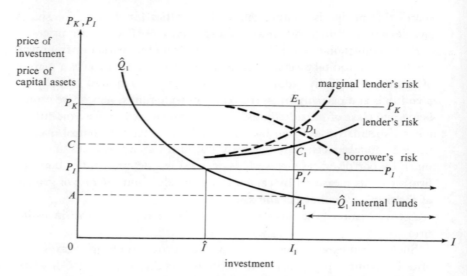

Diagram 5.4   THE FINANCING BEHAVIOR OF A REPRESENTA-
TIVE FIRM

market vicissitudes. When such cash assets are drawn down, the firm
decreases this protection. Analytically, the decrease in such cash buffers
is equivalent to a rise in debts; both changes imply that the set of events
in nature which can seriously affect the firm's ability to meet commitments or carry out plans has increased—the margin of security has decreased.

The firm capitalizes its prospective yields, Q_i—which include dividends, interest, and other cash payments on debt but exclude taxes—at a
rate $\hat{K}$. This places a value on the firm's stock of capital assets, $\hat{P}_{K_i} \cdot K_i$
$= \hat{K}(Q_i)$, which is independent of the firm's financial structure. The firm
also capitalizes its cash-flow commitments, CC, due to debts, dividends,
etc. We assume, in this argument, that the capitalization rate on debts is
also $\hat{K}$, although we really expect the capitalization rate on CC, debts, to
be higher than on Q, prospective yields. This is so because to a borrower
the cash flows on debts, the CC's, are viewed as being certain, whereas
the cash flows from capital assets, the Q's, are uncertain.

For investment to take place it is necessary that $P_{K_i} > K(Q_i)/K_i \geqslant P_I$,
that the price of a unit of capital be greater than or equal to the price

of a unit of investment. In the absence of debt-financing we have $\hat{I} = \hat{Q}_{io}/P_I$. This is the $\hat{I}$ of investment in diagram 5.4.

For capital-asset acquisition to be financed either by retained earnings, $\hat{Q}_i$, or by debt, it is necessary that $\hat{K}(Q_i - CC_i) > 0$. In an abstract, hypothetical world in which the supply of finance to a firm is infinitely elastic, in which all prices and prospective yields are independent of the firm's own scale of operation, and into which the realities of risk and uncertainty never intrude, if the cash flows CC on the debts necessary to finance the acquisition of a unit of capital are less than the prospective yields, then a firm, with such prospects, would want to buy an unlimited—nay, an infinite—amount of capital assets. But vulgar realities in the form of borrower's and lender's risk, let alone monopoly and monopsony positions, intrude, so that even if $\hat{K}(Q - CC) > 0$ the firm will acquire only a limited amount of capital assets.

Borrower's risk has two facets. First, in a world with uncertainty, where the fates of various capital assets and firms can differ, a risk averter will diversify. This means that beyond some point, which for the individual wealth owner or corporation depends upon the size of his wealth, the capitalization rate for any one type of capital asset to be used in a particular line of commerce declines as the amount owned increases. Second, since the borrower sees the cash flows due to debts $(CC\text{'s})$ as certain and the prospective yields $(Q\text{'s})$ as uncertain, increasing the ratio of investment that is debt-financed decreases the margin of security and thus lowers the capitalization rate the borrower applies to the Q's.

Because of borrower's risk, therefore, the demand price for capital assets "falls away" from P_K, and this falling away can be expected to become more precipitous the greater the commitment to this particular type of capital asset and the greater the ratio of borrowed funds. The falling away will normally take place at some point to the right of $\hat{I}$, the amount of investment that can be internally financed, but it may take place to the left of $\hat{I}$. The latter will happen if the view develops that either the inherited commitment to this particular type of capital asset is too great, so that a desire to diversify or to disinvest becomes dominant, or that the inherited balance sheet contains too much debt. These "new" views can arise as a result of events. Symmetrical views can develop favoring more specialization and more debt.

Borrower's risk is subjective; it never appears on signed contracts. It is a focal point for the "quivers and quavers" of uncertainty and the "surprise" of high animal spirits.

Lender's risk does appear on signed contracts. For any set of market conditions, lender's risk, as it applies to a particular firm, takes the form of increased cash-flow requirements in debt contracts, as the ratio of debt to total assets increases. Lender's risk shows up in financial contracts in various forms: higher interest rates, shorter terms to maturity, a requirement to pledge specific assets as collateral, and restrictions on dividend payouts and further borrowing are some of them. Lender's risk rises with an increase in the ratio of debt to equity financing or the ratio of committed cash flows to total prospective cash flows.

In a significant sense, the current supply price of a capital asset to a particular prospective purchaser is not the price per unit at which it is purchased. The supply price is the price at which a producer—or an owner—offers to sell the capital asset plus a capitalized value of the excess of the cash-flow commitments in the financial contract over the commitments which would have been implicit if the investment were internally financed. This "add on" is the capitalized value of the inverse of insurance. The greater the leverage an investing unit uses, i.e., the greater the ratio of debt to internal financing, the greater are such excess contractual cash-flow commitments. Thus the effective P_I curve has a discontinuity at the amount of investment that can be internally financed, $\hat{I}$. After some positive amount of debt-financing the P_I curve can be expected to begin to rise and then to rise at an increasing rate. Furthermore, as the contractual debt ratio rises, all debt issued by the unit will, upon refinancing, have to conform to the marginal contract; thus with a lag a curve marginal to the rising supply curve, the equivalent of a "monoposony" curve, becomes the relevant decision-determining relation which embodies lender's risk.

The fundamental fact about both borrower's and lender's risks is that they reflect subjective valuations. Two entrepreneurs facing identical objective circumstances but having different temperaments would view the borrower's risk quite differently: where one decision-maker will invest, say, I_1, another will extend himself to invest more or be satisfied with less. Lender's risks do lead to observable patterns of borrowing rates, such as those that appear in the "ratings" put on municipal and corporate debt by various services or the premiums over the prime rate that firms have to pay at banks. At any one time, "the market" seems to operate with a consensus about the extent to which operations can be debt-financed for a particular rating, but this consensus can be both stretched and changed: both the acceptable and the actual debt-equity ratios vary in a systematic way over the longer business-cycle swings.

The intersection of the demand curve, allowing for borrower's risk, and the supply curve, adjusted for lender's risk, determines the scale of investment. In diagram 5.4, with the intersection of these supply and demand curves incorporating borrower's and lender's risk at D_1, investment will be I_1, at a price, per unit of capital assets, of P_I. Of the total investment spending of $0P_IP_I'I_1$, $0A$ A_1I_1 will be internally financed and A $P_IP_I'A_1$ will be debt-financed.

Of the prospective yields per unit of capital, the borrowing results in pledged cash flows proportional to A_1C_1/I_1E_1, and the equity owners expect to receive cash flows proportional to $(IA_1 + C_1E_1)/I_1E_1$.

After the capital assets are integrated into the firm's production process, and if these capital assets yield the anticipated Q's, then at the capitalization rate $\hat{K}$, the capital assets $0I_1$ will be valued at P_K. Their total value will be $0P_KE_1I_1$; the investor will have a capital gain. The debts, now more secure, will be generating a cash flow proportional to A_1C_1, but will be capitalized at a lower interest rate than they were initially, for the lender's risk premium will have proven to be excessive. As a result the bond holders will also have a capital gain. The value to the equity owners of their initial investment $\hat{Q}_1$, (equal to $0AA_1I_1$) will be $0AA_1I_1$ plus $CP_KE_1C_1$. This should be reflected in the showing on the exchange of the price of these shares. The existence of lender's risk and borrower's risk as factors limiting investment assures that the successful operation of capital assets will lead to capital appreciation for both the borrower and lender. The Shakespearean dictum "Neither a borrower nor a lender be" fails to take into account the capital gains both parties can enjoy.

The pace of investment is most sensitive to these borrower's and lender's risks. If the curves fall away sharply from the capitalized value of the Q's and rise sharply from the price of investment goods, then investment will be mainly internally financed; if they are shallow rather than steep, the financing of investment will be more heavily levered.

Each period inherits both a liability structure and a set of capital assets from the past. If the repercussions of experience upon preferences and expectations are such that the borrower's and lender's risks are lowered,

so that $I_2 > I_1$ of investment is undertaken for a given $\hat{Q}$, (as is illustrated in diagram 5.5,) then a comparable shift will have to take place in
the acceptable debt-equity ratio for the stock of capital assets owned by
the unit. This will uncover a great deal of ability to finance investment
by borrowing on the basis of ownership of the inherited stock of capital
assets. That is, for the stock of capital assets owned by firms, the ratio of
CC, cash due on debts, to Q, the gross cash flows after taxes, will be low
by the new standards. The leverage of investment financing on expected
earnings can be very high during a period of decreasing risk aversion,
because capital appreciation uncovers borrowing power.

If a decrease in risk aversion affects households that own shares in the
same way that it affects managers and bankers, who effect the shifts in
acceptable debt ratios for investment and capital holdings, then households will become more willing to use more debt to own shares, bankers
will be more willing to finance such "margin" purchases of shares. This
will lead to a rise in share prices. Such a rise in the market price of
equities was interpreted by Keynes as involving "an increase in the
marginal efficiency of the corresponding type of capital" (*GT*, p. 151,
footnote 1), which in the terminology used here raises P_K for given Q's.

Keynes noted that "During a boom the popular estimation of both of
these risks, both borrower's risk and lender's risk, is apt to become

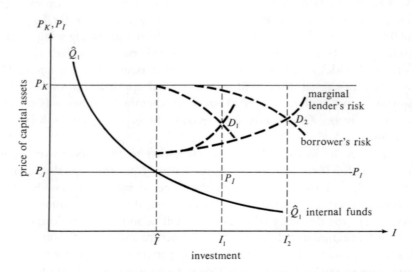

Diagram 5.5 SENSITIVITY OF INVESTMENT TO RISK ESTIMATES

unusually and imprudently low" (*GT*, p. 145). This implies that during a boom the ratio of debt-financing to investment increases: this is borne out by the available data on corporate debt.

AGGREGATE INVESTMENT

The above argument has been for a hypothetical firm or household. We need to aggregate to extend the argument to the economy. We carry over from the earlier analysis the proposition that for a given stock of capital assets, portfolio preferences yield a market price–money supply relation for capital assets in general which is such that the market price of a capital asset is positively related to the quantity of money. This $P_K = P_K(M,Q)$ function has embodied in it the three "slips" identified by Keynes; between money and the interest rate on debts; between the debt interest rate and the marginal efficiency of capital, i.e., the capitalization factors for capital assets; and between the marginal efficiency of capital and the prospective yield on capital assets. Given the quantity of money, this relation determines a demand price for investment goods. The demand curve for capital assets is positively sloped with respect to the supply of money.

Diagram 5.6 illustrates the relation between aggregate investment and finance. The supply curve of investment goods is a rising function of the

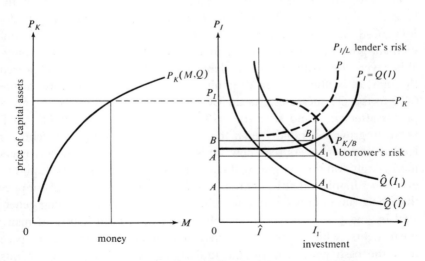

Diagram 5.6 **AGGREGATE INVESTMENT AND FINANCE**

quantity of investment. The anticipated internal funds are given by $\hat{Q}(\hat{I})$. The intersection of P_{IL} and P_{KB}—the supply price of investment goods conditional upon the lender's risk of bankers and the demand price of investment goods conditional upon the borrower's risk of firms— determines the actual pace of investment. Of the total amount spent on investment $0BB_1I_1$, $0AA_1I_1$ are anticipated internal funds and ABB_1A_1 are anticipated borrowed funds.

Let us assume that the financing plan, for the investment of I_1, was based upon the profits firms anticipated they would earn if aggregate income were sufficient to finance an aggregate investment of $\hat{I}$. In fact aggregate investment is I_1, and as this excess investment leads to a higher than anticipated aggregate income, it will also lead to a flow of internal funds of $\hat{Q}(I_1)$, which is greater than anticipated. As a result, after the event, the internal cash flows are such that $0\overset{*}{A}\overset{*}{A}_1I_1$ of the investment is financed internally and $\overset{*}{A}BB_1\overset{*}{A}_1$ is financed externally. In the case illustrated the improvement of realized profits partially frustrates the planned debt-financing of investments of firms and simultaneously reinforces the willingness of firms and bankers to debt-finance further increases in investment. The unused leverage carries over and is available for financing future investment. In addition, as debt charges are lower than anticipated, the share earnings are greater. Equity prices will respond favorably to such increases in the flow of internal funds.

We have constructed a way of looking at investment in which the "popular estimation" of lender's and borrower's risk, which is admittedly influenced by the past performance of the economy, acts as the immediate governor of the pace of investment and thus of the economy. Whenever the willingness to debt-finance increases and is carried through, as is illustrated in diagram 5.5, then the objective ratio of the CC's to the Q's increases. As the CC's rise relative to the Q's, the gross profits after taxes and after the cash commitment due to liabilities will begin to grow less rapidly than the pace of investment and of debt. As lenders and borrowers seek new ways to finance investment, borrowers increasingly, on the margin, will tap sources of funds that value liquidity ever more highly—that is, contract terms on debts will rise. This implies that short-run cash needs due to debts can outrun the cash being generated by the Q's. This is due mainly to the short-term nature of many boom debts, which require the repayment of principal at a faster pace than the cash generated by the underlying operation permits. Units which use this type of debt need to refinance their debt as contracts fall due.

A boom once started lives a precarious life. It depends upon realization of optimistic expectations about yields, so that capital gains accrue to investors in debts and shares as well as to investors in capital assets. From a multitude of possible causes—rising wages or production costs, feedbacks from rising interest rates to the value of older long-term debt, the high cost of refunding previous debt—a large number of units can be forced to try to raise cash at the same time by taking advantage of the liquidity that some of their assets are presumed to have, i.e., by attempting to sell "liquid" assets. Furthermore, for some units the burden of debt in the form of cash commitments can become so large that they are forced to sell or pledge capital assets to acquire cash to meet debt commitments.

This can happen to ordinary firms and to financial organizations.

Assets are liquid so long as there is no preponderance of sellers over buyers. Whenever the need to make position by selling assets becomes quite general, then, unless there is a large standby market supporter, such as a conscientious central bank, asset prices can fall precipitously. When prices of assets—including shares—fall, the corresponding marginal efficiency, or the corresponding demand price of the capital assets, falls too.

In diagram 5.7 the situation after a "crisis," or a reconsideration of the desirable debt structure, is portrayed. With $P_{K_1}(M,Q)$ and M_0 of money

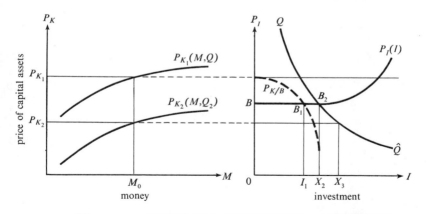

Diagram 5.7   **EFFECT OF A SHIFT IN THE $P_K(M)$ FUNCTION**

the market price of capital assets is high enough so that positive debt-financing could result. However, recent experience has made the potential borrowers view their risk in such a way that only $0I_1$ of investment is desired. This will occur if management begins to view liability structures as being too daring. A conservative restructuring of the balance sheet is then desired; for example, of anticipated internal funds, Q, some $0BB_1I_1$ is to be spent on investment and $I_1B_1B_2X_2$ is to be used to retire debt or acquire financial assets. In this situation, if the income which would generate anticipated internal funds of Q required aggregate investment in excess of I_1, then realized internal funds would be lower than anticipated. The desired improvement in balance sheets will not be realized, and a recursive debt-income deflationary process could be triggered.

If P_{K_2} is the pricing-of-capital-assets relation, all the anticipated internal funds will be used to retire debt or acquire financial assets. As drawn, the maximum $P_{K_2}(M, Q)$ is less than the minimum P_I. Within the set of diagrams used to illustrate the investment relation, this is an illustration of the liquidity trap. The impotence of monetary policy illustrated here does not require that the interest rate on government debt remain constant when the money supply is increased. As illustrated, even if the interest rate on financial assets continues to fall as the supply of money is increased, the capitalization rate applied to investment assets may not rise by enough to induce investment.

◄ 6 ►

Financial Institutions, Financial Instability, and the Pace of Investment

Bankers, both commercial and investment, finance and "broker" the acquisition and control of capital assets by firms, and the "ownership" of firms by households.

There is a multitude of real assets in the world which constitute our capital wealth—buildings, stocks of commodities, goods in course of manufacture and of transport and so forth. The nominal owners of these assets, however, have not infrequently borrowed *money* [Keynes's emphasis] in order to become possessed of them. To a corresponding extent the actual owners of wealth have claims, not on real assets, but on money. A considerable part of this "financing" takes place through the banking system, which imposes its guarantee between its depositors who lend it money and its borrowing customers to whom it loans money with which to finance the purchase of real assets. The interposition of this veil of money between the real asset and the wealth owner is a specially marked characteristic of the modern world.[1]

In servicing firms, banks finance control over real assets; in serving

---

[1]Keynes, "The Consequences to the Banks of the Collapse of Money Value," in *Essays in Persuasion*, Vol. IX, p. 151.

households they both finance and market the acquisition and control of financial assets. In particular, investment bankers administer the distribution and commercial banks finance the ownership of shares. The ownership of the equity interest in a modern corporation is tied into the banking process.

Bankers live in the same expectational climate as the managers of real-capital assets and the households that own shares and other financial assets. The extent to which layering, or leveraging, of retained earnings—i.e., debt-financing—takes place in the financing of investment depends not only on the expectations of investing firms but also on the willingness of bankers to go along with, if not to urge, such layering, as well as on the willingness of households to hold such layered shares at appreciated, even appreciating prices. Whenever firms and households increase such layering, bankers decrease the protection they enjoy from the margin of borrower's investment in whatever is being financed.

An ultimate reality in a capitalist economy is the set of interrelated balance sheets among the various units. Items in the balance sheets set up cash flows. Cash flows are the result of (1) the income-producing system, which includes wages, taxes, and nonfinancial corporate gross profits after taxes, (2) the financial structure, which is composed of as interest, dividends, rents, and repayments on loans, and (3) the dealing or trading in capital assets and financial instruments. For all except dividends, the cash flows determined by the financial structure are contractual commitments.

Transactions in balance-sheet items generate cash flows even as they affect the market price of such assets. This ability to generate cash flows by selling an asset without large price concessions measures the asset's liquidity. Keynes argued that the development of organized security markets was necessary to provide liquidity comparable to that of money for ownership interests, direct or indirect, in capital assets:

> So long as it is open to the individual to employ his wealth in hoarding or lending *money*, the alternative of purchasing actual capital assets cannot be rendered sufficiently attractive (especially to the man who does not manage the capital assets and knows very little about them) except by organising markets wherein these assets can be easily realized for money. [*GT*, pp. 160–61; Keynes's emphasis]

That is, if wealth is owned by any but the actual operators of wealth, then the nonoperating owners will put a premium on the ability to disengage—to sell out, or to redeploy his wealth.

This ability to be exchanged for money at the will of the owner, which is a particular attribute of financial investments, affects the pace of investment:

> The liquidity of investment markets often facilitates though it sometimes impedes the course of new investment. For the fact that each individual investor flatters himself that his commitment is "liquid". . . calms his nerves and makes him much more willing to run a risk. [*GT*, p. 160]

> So far we have had chiefly in mind the state of confidence of the speculator or speculative investor himself and may have seemed to be tacitly assuming that if he himself is satisfied with the prospects, he has unlimited command over money at the market rate of interest. That is, of course, not the case. Thus we must also take account of the other facet of the state of confidence, namely, the confidence of the lending institutions towards those who seek to borrow from them, sometimes described as the state of credit. A collapse in the price of equities, which has had disastrous reactions on the marginal efficiency of capital, may have been due to the weakening either of speculative confidence or of the state of credit. But whereas a weakening of either is enough to assure a collapse, a recovery requires the revival of *both* [Keynes's emphasis]. For whilst the weakening of credit is sufficient to bring about a collapse, its strengthening, though a necessary condition of recovery, is not a sufficient condition. [*GT*, p. 158]

The state of credit reflects bankers' views toward borrowers, and bankers finance the positions of both real-asset holders and equity-share holders. A revision by bankers of their views about the appropriate leverage to use in financing positions in capital assets will not necessarily cause an immediate revision in the market value of these assets— especially if the prospective yields and the capitalization ratio are unaffected. But such a revision of bankers' views can have a strong impact upon equity prices. This is so because the organization of the exchanges is designed to facilitate transactions in equities, which leads to a huge turnover of such indirect investments and a constant revaluation of their market price.

Keynes's remarks about stock exchanges and their impact upon system behavior are particularly relevant to our argument:

> Decisions to invest in private business of the old fashioned type were, however, decisions largely irrevocable, not only for the community as a whole but also for the individual. With the separation between ownership and management which prevails today and with the development of organized investment markets, a new factor of great importance has entered in, which sometimes facilitates investment but sometimes adds greatly to the instability of the system. In the absence of security markets, there is no object in frequently attempting to revalue an investment to which we are committed. But the Stock Exchange re-

values many investments every day and the revaluations give a frequent opportunity to the individual (though not to the community as a whole) to revise his
commitments. . . . But the daily revaluations of the Stock Exchange, though
they are primarily made to facilitate transfers of old investment between one
individual and another, inevitably exert a decisive influence in the rate of current
investment. For there is no sense in building up a new enterprise at a cost greater
than that at which a similar existing enterprise can be purchased; whilst there is
an inducement to spend on a new prospect what may seem an extravagant sum,
if it can be floated off on the Stock Exchange at an immediate profit. Thus
certain classes of investment are governed by the average expectations of those
who deal on the Stock Exchange as revealed in the price of shares, rather than by
the genuine expectations of the professional entrepreneur. [*GT*, p. 150–51]

Keynes distinguishes between enterprise and speculation as follows: he
appropriates

the term *speculation* for the activity of forecasting the psychology of the market
and the term *enterprise* for the activity of forecasting the prospective yields
of [capital?] assets over their whole life. . . . As the organisation of investment
[shares] markets improves, the risk of the predominance of speculation does
however increase. [*GT*, p. 158]

A speculator makes his fortune by correctly betting on the turn of the
market—going long when he expects prices of assets to rise, short when
he expects them to fall. This leads to Keynes's well-known conclusion,
which we cited earlier, that:

Speculators may do no harm as bubbles on a steady stream of enterprise. But
the position is serious when enterprise becomes the bubble on a whirlpool of
speculation. When the capital development of a country becomes a by-product of
the activities of a casino, the job is likely to be ill-done. [*GT*, p. 159]

Whenever, as a result of an improvement in confidence and credit, the
leveraging of investment increases, the owners of the inherited stock of
capital assets, whose liability structure is compatible with a previous
stage of confidence, find themselves with an unused margin of "borrowing power." This margin is as good as retained earnings in providing a
basis for expansion of ownership of capital assets. Thus an increase in
confidence and in the state of credit is equivalent in its effect upon the
potential for debt-financing of investment to an improvement in current
yield. Even if operating firms do not react to such changed views about
the appropriate liability structure, an increase in leveraging can take
place.

Owners and prospective owners of shares can view the debt-financing of share ownership as an alternative to the debt-financing, by the owning organization, of positions in capital assets. Certainly the same changes in the state of confidence that affect the financing of corporations affect the financing of ownership of the shares. (In fact, entrepreneurs, managers, and bankers in their capacity as households are major owners of shares in economies with the distribution of income and wealth that characterizes capitalism.) An increase in borrowing to own shares can be expected to accompany a rise in the willingness to debt-finance capital-asset acquisition. Thus with a fixed supply of shares, the market prices of shares increase.

The finance for both additional capital-asset production and the increased debt-financing of positions has to come from some place. Two sources of such financing may be identified: the creation of money and portfolio diversification of wealth owners, particularly with respect to money holdings but also with respect to shares and capital assets. Keynes noted "that, in general, the banks hold the key position in the transition from a lower to a higher scale of activity."[2]

Bankers can be speculators, just like other business men. In fact, because banker's liabilities are demand, or short-term, deposits and their assets are mainly dated, term, or short loans, bankers are always speculators. They are always speculating in their ability to refinance their positions in assets as withdrawals of deposits take place. Banking as it is practiced could not exist without well-developed loan and security markets among banks.

Bankers speculate also on the composition of their assets. They may very well sell out positions in marketable securities in order to finance additional loans during a boom. But even as bankers sell out securities, the securities must remain within the economic system. This is done by the securities' entering into some non-bank portfolio, as a substitute for cash. For this substitution to take place it must be rendered attractive by higher interest rates. During booms bankers buy back lending ability by selling their investment portfolio to households, corporate holders of cash, and non-bank financial intermediaries.

In the American banking system, banks can raise the ratio of bank liabilities to bank reserves by substituting time for demand deposits, by substituting promises to loan (lines-of-credit) for actual loans, and by

[2]Keynes, "The 'Ex-Ante' Theory of the Rate of Interest," p. 668.

varying the efficiency with which reserves are utilized through interbank transactions in reserves, i.e., transactions in federal funds. Thus the effective quantity of money is endogenously determined. In addition firms can sell their debts, which are called commercial paper, in the open market. This absorbs and activates short-term cash balances of other units. Commercial paper is very much like money as a fine temporary abode of purchasing power, especially as it can be tailor-made to the holders' specifications.

Therefore, the effect of increased external finance is both to increase the money supply and to decrease idle cash balances. In fact velocity changes, if this is an operationally meaningful concept, are the result of such substitutions of short-term debt for monetary assets in portfolios.

During the conglomerate movement in the United States in the 1960s, another aspect of how corporate finance affects the debt structure became evident. The purchase of controlling shares in a takeover is often accomplished by the issuance of a complicated debt-equity-money package by the "buying" firm. After such a takeover the household owner of shares owns a combination of shares and debts in the new corporation in lieu of this share ownership in the old organization. The money that is used in such deals often comes from borrowing and from the "excess" money of either the buying or the bought firms. Examples exist in which the "cash" in the purchased firm's balance sheet was used, by the buyer, to well-nigh pay for the purchase.

Conglomeration of firms may serve one or both of two distinguishable purposes in a world with debt. In one way—the enterprise way—if firm A yields a set of prospective yields Q_A and firm B yields a set of prospective yields Q_B, the enterpriser visualizes that under his direction the new firm $A + B$ will yield Q_{A+B} which is greater than $Q_A + Q_B$. If the excess earnings are sufficiently great, then even a most prudent risk-averting management will be willing to issue debt to finance the takeover.

A speculative takeover might be characterized as follows: Firm A is a debt-financing firm which has cash flows due to debt of C_A such that $C_A/Q_A = \alpha$; firm B, let us say, has eschewed debt-financing: $C_B = 0$. Firm A visualizes that if it is in control of firm B and if the debt ratio of firm A can be applied to firm B's prospective yields, then αQ_B of cash can be raised by debt. This cash can be used for the further expansion of firm $A + B$. Speculative takeovers are based upon the leverage possibilities opened up by the existence of conservative firms, firms whose balance sheets reflect "older" financing practices.

The effect of such portfolio substitutions by both liability issuers and asset holders is to generate, in the aggregate and in the short run, an elastic supply curve of finance. As a boom develops, the supply curve of finance from portfolio substitution is absorbed, and the supply curve of finance may become less elastic. This means that in the early stage of a boom, financing terms do not change much even as debt-financing expands rapidly. In later stages of the boom, financing terms can rise sharply. To the extent that earlier deals were financed with short-term borrowings, such increases in financing charges can feed back upon and adversely affect the value of earlier deals as they are refinanced.

Thus the progress of a boom sees liability experimentation on three levels. Firms engage more heavily in debt-financing, households and firms cut their cash and liquid-asset holdings relative to their debt, and "banks" increase their loans at the expense of the holdings of securities, especially government debt. Furthermore, to an ever-increasing extent banks rely on managing their liabilities so as to accommodate borrowers, and borrowing firms engage in active liability management to finance their asset position.

In fact, the sophistication is carried beyond this when non-bank financial institutions use bank debt, open-market debt, and longer-term bonds to acquire debts. A layering of debts occurs. This debt is built on one main foundation; the quasi-rents, the Q's, earned by business firms in producing income. In addition, in a world where households borrow, another layering of debt exists whose foundation is household income, mainly wages.

The growth of financial intermediation and secondary markets adds other sets of assets that may be held as liquid assets in portfolios; as such they are substitutes for money. Such financial intermediation tends to raise the price of capital assets relative to the price of current output.

Thus speculation has three aspects: (1) the owners of capital-assets speculate by debt-financing investment and positions in the stock of capital-assets; (2) banks and other financial institutions speculate on the asset mix they own and on the liability mix they owe; (3) firms and households speculate on the financial assets they own and on how they finance their position in these assets.

During a boom the speculative demand for money decreases, and portfolios become more heavily weighted with debt-financed positions. Owners of capital assets commit larger portions of their expected cash flows from operations, their Q's, to the payment of financial commitments, CC. Banks increase their ownership of loans at the expense of investments, and by active liability management increase their scale of operations for given cash reserves. Other financial institutions also increase their scale of operations by actively pursuing funds. Households and firms substitute nonmoney financial assets for money as their liquid reserves.

Units, both operating and financial, with elaborated liability structures develop cash-payment commitments which exceed the cash receipts they will get over the short period from contracts they own, or from operations. To fulfill their cash-payment commitments, they must refinance by selling either their assets or their liabilities. Some financial assets and liabilities have markets which are broad, with many participants, and deep, in the sense that small price concessions will bring forth a large increment of funds, i.e., an elastic supply of finance. Other financial markets are narrow, with only a few participants, and shallow, so that any spurt in the amount offered will lead to large price declines, without any commensurate increase in the supply of funds.

The process of selling financial assets or liabilities to fulfill cash-payment commitments is called "position making," the position being the unit's holdings of assets which, while they earn income, do not possess markets in which they can be readily sold. For corporations the "position" which has to be financed is in the capital assets necessary for production; for financial firms, the "position" is defined by the assets with poor secondary markets.

As a boom develops households, firms, and financial institutions are forced to undertake ever more adventuresome position-making activity. When the limit of their ability to borrow from one to repay another is reached, the option is to either sell out some position or to bring to a halt, or slow down, asset acquisition. For operating firms this involves a reduction in the leverage used in financing new investment. In diagram 6.1 desired investment for a firm shifts from I_1 to I_2 as firms and bankers become more optimistic and from I_2 to I_1 as firms and bankers become less optimistic, more constrained by financing conditions.

When the speculative demand for money increases, owing to an increase in the danger seen as arising from liability structures, then firms,

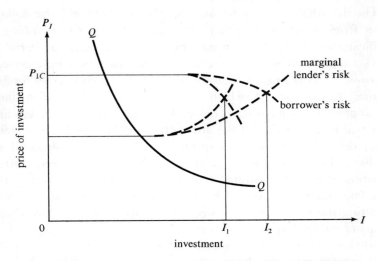

Diagram 6.1   *FINANCING CONDITIONS AND INVESTMENT*

households, and financial institutions try to sell or reduce their assets to repay debts. This leads to a fall in the price of assets. A drop in the $P_K(M, Q)$ function (diagram 6.2) from P_{K_1} to P_{K_2} will take place; this is what happens in a crisis. A decline in share prices is one aspect of a crisis situation.

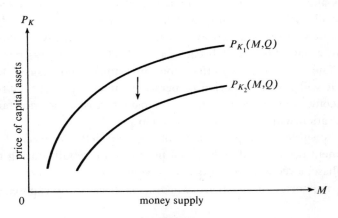

Diagram 6.2   *THE P_K-MONEY RELATION*

The debt-deflation process, such as Fisher described,[3] that follows a crisis arises out of two situations. In diagram 6.3 one situation for a firm is illustrated. Here the demand price of capital assets as derived by market capitalization of quasi-rents is greater than the supply price, but borrower's risk is so great that investment is less than internal funds can finance. In diagram 6.4, which illustrates the second situation, the demand price of capital assets is below the supply price; investment in this case will tend to zero. All the internally generated funds are utilized to repay debt. A major objective of business, bankers, and financial intermediaries in this situation is to clean up their balance sheets. Often in situations like those illustrated in diagrams 6.3 and 6.4, firms will also be "funding" their short-term debt, i.e., issuing long-term debt to replace maturing short-term debt. In this way the near-term cash-flow commitments of the liability structure can be reduced. Such refunding can tend to sustain, and may even raise, long-term interest rates even as short-term interest rates are decreasing: banks can have lending ability and borrowers, as well as bankers, may be unwilling to put it to use.

With diagrams 6.3 and 6.4 we are no longer in a boom; we are in a debt-deflation process. A feedback from the purely financial developments to the demand-for-investment output, and by way of the multiplier to the demand-for-consumption output, takes place. Unemployment and a depression result.

The combined effect of the short-run stabilizing properties of consumption expenditures, the stabilizing properties of government expenditures and tax schedules, the influence of those monetary assets which are not the debt of any unit, and the central bank acting as a lender of last resort will bring a debt-deflation and its accompanying income decline to a halt. However, because a debt-deflation process has both an immediate and a lingering effect upon investment and desired debt positions, it will lead to a period of persistent unemployment. A relatively low-income, high-unemployment, stagnant recession of uncertain depth and duration will follow a debt-deflation process.

As the subjective repercussions of the debt-deflation wear off, as disinvestment occurs, and as financial positions are rebuilt during the stagnant phase, a recovery and expansion begins. Such a recovery starts with strong memories of the penalty extracted because of exposed liability

[3]See Fisher, "The Debt-Deflation Theory of Great Depressions."

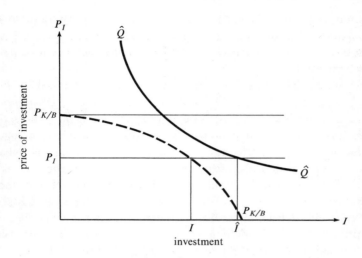

Diagram 6.3   BORROWER'S RISK AND DEBT DEFLATION

positions during the debt-deflation and with liability structures that have
been purged of debt. However, success breeds daring, and over time
the memory of the past disaster is eroded. Stability—even of an
expansion—is destabilizing in that more adventuresome financing of investment pays off to the leaders, and others follow. Thus an expansion
will, at an accelerating rate, feed into the boom.

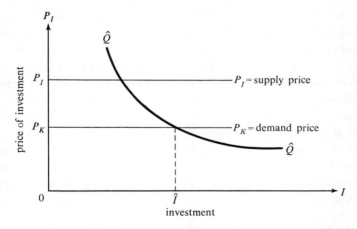

Diagram 6.4   SUPPLY PRICE GREATER THAN DEMAND PRICE

Thus within a capitalist economy, Keynes observed, "It is to an important extent, the 'financial' facilities that regulate the *pace* of new investment";[4] and it is the pace of investment that determines income and employment.

Keynes wrote that in dealing with uncertainty, "In practice we have tacitly agreed, as a rule to fall back on what is, in truth, a *convention*" *(GT*, p. 152; Keynes's emphasis). But in a capitalist economy the aspect which is least bound by technology or by fundamental psychological properties, which is most clearly a convention or even a fashion, subject to moods of optimism and pessimism and responsive to the visions of soothsayers, is the liability structure of both operating and financial organizations. In economies where borrowing and lending exist, ingenuity goes into developing and introducing financial innovations, just as into production and marketing innovations. Financing is often based upon an assumption "that the existing state of affairs will continue indefinitely" *(GT*, p. 152), but of course this assumption proves false. During a boom the existing state is the boom with its accompanying capital gains and asset revaluations. During both a debt-deflation and a stagnant recession the same conventional assumption of the present always ruling is made; the guiding wisdom is that debts are to be avoided, for debts lead to disaster. As a recovery approaches full employment the current generation of economic soothsayers will proclaim that the business cycle has been banished from the land and a new era of permanent prosperity has been inaugurated. Debts can be taken on because the new policy instruments—be it the Federal Reserve System or fiscal policy —together with the greater sophistication of the economic scientists advising on policy assure that crises and debt-deflations are now things of the past. But in truth neither the boom, nor the debt deflation, nor the stagnation, and certainly not a recovery or full-employment growth can continue indefinitely. Each state nurtures forces that lead to its own destruction.

Of all the markets in the economy, the markets for investments and the debt instruments used to acquire shares and control over capital assets are most clearly based upon tenuous conventions. It is therefore "not surprising that a convention, in an absolute view of things so arbitrary, should have its weak points. It is its precariousness which creates

---

[4]Keynes, "Alternative Theories of the Rate of Interest," p. 248.

no small part of our contemporary [1935] problem of securing sufficient investment" (*GT*, p. 153).

The conclusion to our argument is that the missing step in the standard Keynesian theory was the explicit consideration of capitalist finance within a cyclical and speculative context. Once capitalist finance is introduced and the development of cash flows (as stated in the interrelated balance sheets) during the various states of the economy is explicitly examined, then the full power of the revolutionary insights and the alternative frame of analysis that Keynes developed becomes evident.

Why the financial aspects were left essentially implicit, why they were subject to allusion rather than detailed argumentation in *The General Theory*, I do not know. Perhaps, as Joan Robinson suggested, Keynes was like a snake shedding his skin as he was writing *The General Theory*, and the book was written when the old skin—the classical view—was not fully off. Thus Keynes in *The General Theory* did not emerge with a full-blown cyclical and financial analysis and a critique of capitalism. Enough of the barter paradigm remained in his thinking so that he did not make the final step to an analysis of the capitalist process that is fully rooted in "the City" and "Wall Street."

Even though we may be unable to explain why Keynes did not expand upon his reference to finance, we may offer a reason why succeeding generations did not follow the hints. First, as was mentioned earlier, the problems of the period from the appearance of *The General Theory* until the recent past, say the middle 1960s, were characterized by robust finance. The speculative fevers that had characterized previous explosions into booms was missing. The banking system came out of the war with a portfolio heavily weighted with government debt, and it was not until the 1960s that banks began to speculate actively with respect to their liabilities. It was a unique period in which finance mattered relatively little; at least, finance did not interpose its destabilizing ways.

Furthermore, government, unfortunately due to continued massive military spending, remained big, and taxes, heavily weighted with income and employment taxes, were high and responsive to changes in income. Thus a high floor to income due to government spending and a fiscal constraint against undue expansion due to the tax system were operative. Even after the crunch of 1966, the liquidity squeeze of 1969–70, the devaluations of 1971 and 1973, and the persistence of inflation, it remains true that the combination of structural changes, particularly the relative size of the government, and more sophisticated policy operations has changed the shape, though not the essential character, of capitalist business cycles.

One last reason may be advanced as to why Keynes's emphasis upon finance in *The General Theory* was not followed as economics developed after World War II. The analytical economists did not have Keynes's exposure to the operations of the City—or Wall Street. In the period after World War II, careers of economists were made by combinations of purely academic work and government service. The knowledgeable view of the operation of finance that Keynes possessed was not readily available to academic economists, and those knowledgeable about finance did not have the skeptical, aloof attitude toward capitalist enterprise necessary to understand and appreciate the basically critical attitude that permeated Keynes's work.

Thus the message was neglected: it is finance that acts as the sometimes dampening, sometimes amplifying governor for investment. As a result, finance sets the pace for the economy.

‹ 7 ›

Some Implications of the Alternative Interpretation

INTRODUCTION

In chapters 3 to 6 an interpretation of *The General Theory* has been put forth that rests upon Keynes's theory of investment and finance. This interpretation is an alternative to today's conventional wisdom, which holds that the valuable insights of *The General Theory* have been incorporated into the neoclassical synthesis. However, whereas the neoclassical synthesis leads to propositions that the normal path of a market economy can be characterized as one of full-employment growth, the alternative interpretation leads to propositions that the normal path of a capitalist economy is cyclical; that is, the normal path can be characterized as a succession of system states. Thus, the two interpretations of Keynes lead to substantially different views of the normal functioning of a capitalist economy.

In the alternative interpretation, the core of Keynes's system consists of an analysis of capitalist finance in the context of uncertainty, and of how capitalist finance affects the valuation of items in the stock of capital assets and thus affects the pace of investment. This core of Keynesian economics is fundamentally inconsistent with the static-production-function and invariant-preference-system constructs which are the basis of the neoclassical synthesis. Keynes and the neoclassical view blend only if one or the other is distorted. In the neoclassical synthesis, Keynes has been distorted.

In Keynes's theory, investment is the proximate tune caller for aggregate demand. In Keynes's asset-valuation model, productive capital assets are perhaps best viewed as another, albeit peculiar, speculative financial asset. The peculiarity of capital assets as financial assets is due to the thinness of many of the resale markets for such assets and to the fact that yields which a capital asset will earn are contingent both upon the performance of a particular firm, operating in a defined market, and upon the overall cyclical behavior of the economy.

In portfolio terms, the production of an increment to the capital stock is equivalent to the creation of an addition to the stock of financial assets. However, whereas the production of an addition to the stock of ordinary financial assets does not generate a significant demand for labor or increase productive capacity, investment requires the employment of labor and increases productive capacity. In addition, investment must be financed. This implies that investment leaves behind a residue of proper financial instruments.

In this chapter we will look at some implications of the alternative interpretation. Investment demand, which typically, in the aggregate, requires external financing, and consumption demand, which in the first instance can be assumed to be financed by wages and household dividend and interest receipts, will be looked at as budget constraints. In the standard microeconomic analysis of producers' and consumers' choice, a production function or a preference system is combined with a budget constraint to yield the combination of goods produced and used. However, the question, "What determines the budget constraints?" is rarely asked, and if asked the answer is often an evasion. At the level of price theory, the way in which banking and financial relations affect what is spent is ignored. Inasmuch as the effective demand for current output by a sector is determined not only by the current income flows and current external finance but also by the sector's cash-payment commitments due to past debt, the alternative interpretation can be summarized as a theory of the determination of the effective budget constraints. The economics of the determination of the budget constraint logically precedes and sets the stage for the economics of the selection of particular items of investment and consumption.

Our model of the investment process focused on two markets and the way in which they are linked by finance. One market determined the demand price for capital assets, the other gave us the supply price of investment output, and the financial markets linked the two by determining both the position of the schedule that gives us the demand price for capital assets and the terms on which investment goods can be financed. In our argument to date, the first schedule shifted as uncertainty and financial market developments affected portfolio possibilities and preferences, whereas the schedule for investment-goods output was assumed fixed. In this chapter we will investigate how the schedule for investment-goods output shifts as the money-wage rate and what Keynes called user cost change and apply our results to deflationary and inflationary processes.

THE ECONOMICS OF BUDGET CONSTRAINTS

For a private and closed economy, in which government and foreign demand can be ignored, total final demand, or income, is equal to the sum of consumption and investment demand; $Y = C + I$. It is this aggregate demand which enters into the inverse of the supply function to determine the level of employment. This inverse reading of the supply function as an employment function was discussed in chapter 2.

Consumption demand is passive. Within the cyclical context it mainly depends upon income; that is, $C = C(Y)$. Income in the context of a closed economy, with no government and no foreign sectors, is equal to the wage bill plus profits. In a cash-flow oriented analysis it is best to interpret profits as gross profits, investment as gross investment, and thus income as gross national product.

If we assume that no installment credit arrangements exist and that workers' incomes are not so generous or secure that workers succeed in accumulating financial resources, then workers' consumption will equal workers' wages: this assumption is not necessary—only convenient.

Gross profit income (the quasi-rents of our prior argument) is in part retained, in part used to pay contractual debts and debt charges, and in part paid out as dividends and interest. Retained earnings are the internal funds (the $\hat{Q}$ of our prior argument) which can be levered by debt to finance the acquisition of additional capital assets—either from the stock of existing capital assets or by the production of investment output. Dividends and interest charges paid by firms, D (equal to $Q - \hat{Q}$), are household income which can finance consumption demand. We assume that some portion of these financial returns are so used. The remainder of the nonwage income of households is used to acquire financial assets.

Gross earnings minus taxes and payment of interest on financial instruments are the retained earnings, the $\hat{Q}$'s, of our prior argument. These become the base for the debt-financing of investment, or alternatively are available to lower outstanding debts or to acquire financial investments. Investment is some variable debt-ratio multiplier of the amount that anticipated gross retained earnings can finance. Thus, investment demand consists of two parts, the amount that can be financed by the internal funds and the amount that is financed by debts. The budget constraint for investment is

$$I = (1 + \lambda) \hat{Q}; \quad \lambda > 0 \text{ in a normal expansion}$$
$$\lambda > > 0 \text{ in a boom}$$
$$\lambda \leq 0 \text{ in a recession}$$
$$\lambda < < 0 \text{ in a debt deflation}$$

where $\hat{Q}$ is the period's retained earnings and λ is a variable debt-ratio multiple on retained earnings (the symbols, $> >$ and $< <$ indicate "very much" greater and "very much" smaller): $\lambda \hat{Q}$ is the external finance.

The budget constraint for household consumption expenditure is:

$$C - W + \alpha D,$$

where α is the proportion of household income from owning capital that is spent.

The total budget constraint is the sum of consumption plus investment budgets:

$$Y = W + \alpha D + (1 + \lambda) \hat{Q}.$$

Of the household income received $(1 - \alpha)D$ is not used to finance consumption. By intermediation, some portion of household saving is made available to finance investment. We will write that as $u(1 - \alpha)D$, so that $(1 - u)(1 - \alpha)D$ is the incremental portfolio demand for money by households. As the households with capital income are the only households with portfolios of financial assets, u gives us the incremental portfolio demand for money. We can assume that incremental demand equals the average demand for money in portfolios; furthermore, in any broader argument u is a variable related both to the state of uncertainty and the rate of interest on money loans.

If $\lambda \hat{Q} > u(1 - \alpha)D$, then some of investment will have to be financed in a manner other than by the intermediation of household savings. This excess $\left[\lambda \hat{Q} - u(1 - \alpha)D\right]$ of investment financing demanded over the supply available from intermediation of savings can be satisfied by some combination of an increase in the money supply and of a decrease in the money holdings in portfolios, i.e., by an increase in velocity. But the way in which the money supply responds to financing demand and the way in which portfolios respond to financial market conditions (as well as the way in which the levering of internal funds behaves as uncertainty and financial market conditions change) are the essence of the Keynesian theory of investment.

If we translate the accounting relations we have just examined into the arbitrary ex-ante–ex-post analysis which is sometimes used in expositions of the simple aggregate models, we can examine a bit more closely how investment and monetary changes call the tune for income determination. Let us write planned consumption at any date, t, as being due to the previous period's income of households from wages and capital,

$$C_{t \text{ ex ante}} = W_{t-1} + \alpha D_{t-1}$$

and planned investment as retained earnings plus a leverage factor,

$$I_{t \text{ ex ante}} = (1 + \lambda)\hat{Q}_{t-1} \quad \text{so that}$$

$$Y_{t \text{ ex ante}} = W_{t-1} + \alpha D_{t-1} + \hat{Q}_{t-1} + \lambda \hat{Q}_{t-1}.$$

As

$$Y_{t-1 \text{ ex post}} = W_{t-1} + D_{t-1} + \hat{Q}_{t-1}$$

$$Y_{t \text{ ex ante}} > Y_{t-1 \text{ ex post}} \quad \text{as} \quad \alpha D_{t-1} + \lambda \hat{Q}_{t-1} > D_{t-1}$$

or

$$\lambda \hat{Q}_{t-1} > (1 - \alpha)D_{t-1}.$$

Thus for income to increase, the externally financed investment must exceed the savings of households. Inasmuch as u percent of household savings is presumed to be made available for financing investment, we have that

$$\lambda \, \hat{Q}_{t-1} = \Delta M_t + u \, (1 - \alpha) D_{t-1}$$

so that $\Delta M_t > (1 - \alpha) D_{t-1} - u \, (1 - \alpha) D_{t-1}$

$$\Delta M_t > (1 - u) \, (1 - \alpha) D_{t-1} \quad \text{for}$$

$$Y_{t \text{ ex ante}} > Y_{t-1 \text{ ex post}}$$

where ΔM_t can be either money creation or a change in velocity.

What we have is the bare bones of a model in which the path of income, in the sense of the aggregate budget constraint, depends crucially upon two phenomena: the determination of total investment demand, $(1 + \lambda)\hat{Q}$, and the external financing of investment through monetary changes, ΔM. Thus, it is the views of businessmen and bankers about the appropriate financial relations that call the tune for aggregate demand and employment. These views are volatile, responding to the past of the economy, and they change as the economy transits among the various types of behavior (boom, crisis, debt-deflation, stagnation, and relatively steady expansion) which characterize the performance of capitalism.

DEFLATION AND INFLATION IN AN ECONOMY WITH CAPITALIST FINANCE

The Keynesian theory of investment rests upon two basic constructs: the portfolio relation, which relates the demand price for capital assets to the structure of business, household, and banker's portfolios, and the supply function for investment output, which relates the supply price to the pace of production of investment output. Financing conditions for capital-asset holdings and investment demand, which depend upon the views of businessmen and bankers with respect to both borrower's and lender's uncertainty, link the demand price for capital assets and the supply price of investment output.

To this point, we have focused upon the way uncertainty affects the position of the relation which determines the demand price for capital assets and the extent to which internal funds and net worth are levered.

The supply function for investment output has been assumed to be fixed. We will now examine how money wages and what Keynes called user cost determine the position on the price-of-investment, quantity-of-investment plane of the supply function of investment output. In Keynes's view, the money-wage rate and the user cost are determinants of the position of the supply schedule of output, so that changes in these costs are the proximate determinant of the price level. Furthermore, in a world where the past and the future are always present in the form of inherited and currently created financial commitments, wage deflations and inflations are destabilizing and self-sustaining processes. Thus, for example, the remedy of wage deflation for unemployment, which is often advanced by classical economists and which is enshrined in the real-balance effects of the neoclassical synthesis, will tend to make unemployment worse, not better.

Thus, once money-wage rates and user costs are introduced into the supply functions for investment and consumers' goods, we can examine the nature and repercussions of wage deflation and inflation. The futility of wage deflation in eliminating unemployment and the key role of the money-wage rate in the production of investment goods in generating inflation become apparent. In particular, if economic policy depends upon investment to sustain full employment and if the money-wage rate in investment-goods production increases, then monetary and fiscal policy will be accommodating rather than initiating influences upon prices. The initiating influence is in the wage-determination process.

Revenue from the sale of output can be broken into three components: labor costs, costs of purchased materials, and rents earned by the capital assets. In determining his supply or offer price for output, an entrepreneur will require that this price exceed the marginal labor costs plus marginal material costs by some standard. This standard or minimum acceptable expected quasi-rent is what Keynes called user costs: user cost is defined as "the reduction in the value of equipment due to using it as compared with not using it. . . . It must be arrived at, therefore, by calculating the discounted value of the additional prospective yield which could be obtained at some later date if it [the equipment] were not used now" (*GT*, p. 70).

User cost therefore brings depreciation and a variant of the normal or expected profit rate into the determination of supply price. The assumption underlying the doctrine of user cost is that if a capital asset is used in producing output today, it will not be available to produce output at some future date. Furthermore, it is assumed that at some future date, capital assets of the general type now being used will be produced, and this will take place only if the quasi-rents that this capital asset is expected to yield, discounted at a positive interest rate, exceed the supply price of the capital asset. The expectation is that if the services of a capital asset are not used today, they will earn these quasi-rents in the future. The present value of these future quasi-rents is the minimum quasi-rent that will be acceptable now, and the supply price of output will include this return. The minimum acceptable quasi-rent is equivalent to a reservation price. The market quasi-rent will not fall below this level. The minimum acceptable quasi-rent is determined by the level of quasi-rents that will draw forth production of the investment output, the expected date in the future at which such quasi-rents will be earned, and the discount rate applied to the expected quasi-rent. Note that if a firm is under a severe liquidity bind, then the discount rate applied to future returns will be very high. As a result, any positive current quasi-rent will lead to the use of the capital asset. The supply schedule for output reflects not only the cyclical behavior of the economy but also the current financial climate.

If a capital asset does not waste with use (if it conforms to the definition of Ricardian "land" in being some original and indestructible producing power) then it is a pure-rent-yielding asset in the sense that the expected income and the replacement cost do not determine the amount of the services supplied. Pure rent results when a capital asset is scarce. In a cyclical economy, the relative scarcity of capital assets at any time depends upon the cyclical stage of the economy; however, with assets that waste, the reservation quasi-rent will lead to various amounts of the capital asset being withheld from use. The fundamental unemployment is that of capital assets.

If we assume fixed proportions in production, then the amount of capital services entrepreneurs wish to use also determines the amount of labor they wish to employ. Whereas capital services not used today will be available some other day, labor services not used are lost forever. Cyclical unemployment is more due to the total demand being insufficient to yield large enough quasi-rents then it is due to wage income not meeting some standard.

Given that there is no reservation price for labor except for the costs of the journey to work, the excess supply of labor when capital services are being reserved should, if market processes function, lead to declining money wages. A decline in money wages lowers the supply curve for consumption output, but it also lowers wage incomes for any volume of employment. A decline in money wages also lowers the expected replacement costs for capital assets at the date the redundancy is expected to be eliminated. Therefore, if the discount rate does not change, the user-cost component of the supply price will also fall. If the dollar amount of investment-good purchases financed by monetary changes (ΔM) does not change, then real investment might well increase. This rise in real investment will, by way of the multiplier, raise income until the income is attained at which savings out of retained earnings plus the savings out of dividends and interest equals the new investment.

The critical assumption in the above argument is that the demand for investment goods financed by monetary changes does not decline as the money-wage rate declines. Falling wage rates mean that if workers are to buy the same real output, the quasi-rents will need to fall along with wages. However, we are dealing with an economy where external finance and thus debts exist. The expected quasi-rents are the source of funds that enables the commitments on inherited as well as newly created debt to be met. As the contractual commitments on inherited debt do not decline as wage income and quasi-rents fall, the proportion of wage incomes and quasi-rents committed by contracts increases: the burden of debt increases in a deflation. Under these circumstances, we can expect the willingness to go into debt to finance investment to decrease; the purchases of investment goods that are financed by monetary changes will decline.

Furthermore, as prices and wages fall, the realization spreads that speculative capital gains can be earned by holding money: velocity will tend to decline. Instead of levering retained quasi-rents to finance investment, firms will use retained quasi-rents to decrease debts (λ of the preceding section becomes less than zero). A wage deflation can be expected to lead to a fall in real investment below the level at which the initial excess supply of labor existed. Downward wage flexibility, in a situation with unemployment, will make things worse.

In an economy where the need to maintain a close approximation to full employment is taken seriously by the public authorities, and where the basic strategy of the full-employment policy is to sustain private-sector investment, a rise in the supply price of investment goods, due to a rise in money-wage rates in the industries producing investment goods (primarily construction), will generalize into an equivalent rise in all prices and money wages. An inflationary process in a full-employment, investment-oriented economy may well be initiated by the process which determines money wages in the investment-goods industries and will be generalized to other markets by the monetary and fiscal reactions undertaken to sustain full employment.

For private investment to be sustained in the face of upward shifts in the supply schedule of investment goods, it is necessary that either the expected quasi-rents rise or the discount rate applicable to such quasi-rents fall. As was noted in our earlier argument, as an economy moves toward full employment and then sustains full employment for a time, both these reactions take place. This is so because the view that cycles are a thing of the past, so that future quasi-rents will now on the average be both larger and more assured, becomes prevalent. Thus it is possible for the relation between the price of capital assets and the supply price of investment to be conducive to sustained or even increasing investment as the supply price of investment increases.

However, once the cyclical impact upon the expected quasi-rents and the effective capitalization rate are absorbed, further increases in the supply price of investment, due to money-wage increases, will need to be offset by raising quasi-rents, either as a proportion of full-employment income or as a result of a constant percentage markup on rising labor costs in all output. Inasmuch as there are limits to the extent to which quasi-rents can be increased as a proportion of income, increases in labor costs in investment production in a full-employment economy must be ratified by a generalized inflation.

The need for generalized inflation, in an economy where full employment is maintained by private investment, is evident from the way in which such private investment is financed in a sustained full-employment economy. Not only is an increasing proportion of private investment financed by debt during such a process, but positions in the inherited stock of private investment are increasingly financed by debt. In fact, one way in which the capitalized value of the quasi-rents is kept in step with the rising supply price of investment output is by increasing the amount of debt-financing of positions in the stock of capital assets. As the cash-flow commitments embodied in debts are met out of the quasi-rents, both bankers and businessmen will go along with the increased ratio of debt to internal financing of investment only if they are reasonably confident that the quasi-rents will grow, i.e., if they believe inflation will take place.

The implications of rising wages in the investment-goods industries upon investment can be illustrated by the type of diagram we have used earlier (see diagram 7.1). With the initial supply curve for investment goods, S_1-S_1, $\bar{I}_1$ of investment can be financed internally and presumably I_1 of investment will take place with I_1-$\bar{I}_1$ externally financed. If wages in investment goods increase so that the supply schedule becomes S_2-S_2, then, with $\hat{Q}_1$ of internal funds, $\bar{I}_2$ can be financed internally and presumably $\bar{I}_2$ will be the total investment. If I_1 is the amount of investment required by full employment, then for full employment to persist the price of items in the stock of capital assets will need to rise above P_{K_1}, and this will occur only if either interest rates fall or the expected quasi-rents increase.

This is so because if I_1 is to be put into place with internal funds restricted to $\hat{Q}_1$, the amount and the proportion of external financing will need to increase: that is, whereas I_1-$\bar{I}_1$ of investment was externally financed in the initial situation, with the supply schedule S_2, I_1-$\bar{I}_2$ of investment will need to be externally financed if full employment is to persist. In order to achieve this larger amount of external financing, the

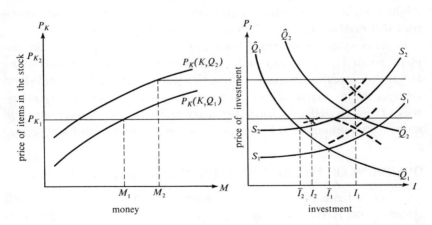

Diagram 7.1   MONEY   WAGES   IN   INVESTMENT   GOODS   AND
              INVESTMENT

monetary authorities will have to make sure that the banking system can expand loans. Thus, an increase of M beyond M_1 will be needed. The increase in the money value of debt-financed investment and the increase in money supply relative to the value of capital assets means that demand for consumption goods and the demand for labor in consumption-goods production increases. This leads to higher wages as well as higher quasi-rents in consumption-goods production: a generalized inflationary process is set off by the combination of money-wage increases in the production of investment goods and the commitment to maintain investment in order to maintain full employment. This results in an upward shift of the P_K relation to $P_K(K, \hat{Q}_2)$. Presumably, with a money supply of M_2 and the $P_K(K, \hat{Q}_2)$ relation, conditions conducive to the financing of I_1 of investment are reestablished.

If the monetary stimulus is not enough to bring forth the required amount of investment, then some combination of government spending or tax cuts will be required to maintain full employment. In a contract-investment oriented economy, the government spending will be heavily investment, and the tax cuts will likely be of an investment-stimulating character (i.e., one which increases the gross retained earnings after taxes of firms). In either case, debt-financing and money creation will take place, a process which again feeds into the demand for consumption labor and tends to raise wages in consumption-goods production. Thus, no matter which path the accommodating monetary and fiscal policy might take, an initial inflationary push in the investment-goods industries will need to be generalized into an economy-wide inflation.

In an economy with strong trade unions in the production of investment goods (construction) and a policy commitment to maintain the output of investment goods, the effective determinant of price-level changes is the course of money wages in the investment-goods industries. Thus, any effective antiinflationary policy in such an economy will require institutional controls on money-wage changes in this key sector.

OVERVIEW OF THE ALTERNATIVE INTERPRETATION

Basic to the alternative interpretation is the view that each system state is transitory and carries with it financial developments which assure the succession of another system state. In this interpretation the boom is critical; it builds an ever-more-demanding liability structure on the base of a cash-flow foundation consisting of the prospective yields of capital assets, which are, because of technology and the limited ability to squeeze workers' real wages, at best constrained ultimately to grow at a steady rate in real terms. The debt base, which grows at an accelerating rate during a boom, is not so constrained. Thus, debts require increased servicing as they grow and as financing charges increase. Realized quasi-rents which ultimately in real terms can grow at only a steady rate become in these circumstances an inadequate source of the cash that debt servicing requires.

The addition of layered financial intermediation to the financing process adds further speculative elements. The speculative aspect of banking is inherent in the very process of lending long and borrowing short. However, in a boom the ingenuity of bankers is directed at turning every possible source of temporarily idle cash into a source of financing for either real operations or financial position making. The tendency therefore is to generate endogenously a structure of cash-payment commitments which embodies an ever-closer articulation of cash payment and receipts, and in which an ever-larger portion of units is forced to refinance debts when due. Thus units become ever more dependent upon the normal functioning of financial as well as product and factor markets. A sharp change occurs when position making by refinancing breaks down; the change leads to a sharp downward shift in the $P_K(M)$ function and a sharp rise in borrower's and lender's risk. In these circumstances, the pace of investment can, and does, quickly slow down.

We have tried to make explicit a model of system behavior which is consistent with the emphasis that Keynes placed in *The General Theory* upon both the cyclical and the financial nature of the capitalism he was examining. This interpretation of Keynes makes *The General Theory* consistent with views that were widespread in the early 1930s: that what had gone wrong had its roots in the imperfections of the monetary-financial system. The greatness of *The General Theory* was that Keynes visualized these as systemic rather than accidental or perhaps incidental attributes of capitalism. He recognized that the problems of such an economy—one with a systemic flaw—could not be diagnosed, let alone prescribed for, if the theory being applied did not recognize that the problem existed. Only a theory that was explicitly cyclical and overtly financial was capable of being useful.

Whereas the perceptive monetary economists of his day, such as H.

Simons, J. Viner, and D. Robertson, were trying to add to a traditional classical model—whose primary focus was resource allocation—realistic financial bright-work, Keynes broke with tradition and directly introduced financial considerations as primary determinants of the various sectoral budget constraints. In both the Hicks-Hansen model and the neoclassical synthesis this emphasis upon the determinants of demand, and in particular the integration of money with investment demand, has proved to be a more powerful tool of analysis and a better guide to policy than the classical models, even though the full power of Keynes's insights was not integrated into the formal models that have become the conventional wisdom. From the point of view of these conventional models recent experience has had anomalous characteristics. However, those aspects of Keynes's perspective which we have stressed, but which were ignored in developing the standard interpretation, can handle these apparent anomalies. Unreconstructed Keynesianism is more relevant to today's situation than the conventional wisdom, and furthermore has policy implications that go beyond the standard guidelines for fiscal and monetary policy.

· 8 ·

Social Philosophy and Economic Policy

INTRODUCTION

The last chapter of *The General Theory* carries the long but diffident title, "Concluding Notes on the Social Philosophy Towards Which The General Theory Might Lead." Keynes was a political animal throughout his life. He had a continuing association with the Liberal Party, both in its period of ascendency prior to World War I and in its decline after that war. In an interpretation of Keynes's views on the implications of *The General Theory* for broader social issues and on the appropriate structure of policies designed to implement the new theory, his writings on politics and social policy prior to *The General Theory* are relevant. While *The General Theory* marks a sharp break in economic theory, the "social philosophy" implications he drew from the work are consistent with his earlier views. In fact, *The General Theory* can be viewed as giving an economic theoretic rationalization for views that Keynes's ethics and intuition had led him to, even as he was a practicing "classical" economist.

In an essay on "The End of Laissez-Faire" written in 1926, Keynes notes that, "At present, our sympathy and our judgements are liable to be on different sides, which is a painful and paralysing state of mind."[1] Even as he was attempting to adjust standard economic theory to the realities and problems of the world as he saw them, in his political and economic writings of the 1920s he regularly advocated economic policies that were inconsistent with the implications that the majority of his colleagues were drawing from economic theory. The public-policy inferences he drew from *The General Theory* were consistent with these earlier views, as is the book's social philosophy, as stated in its final chapter.

The argument in this chapter is divided into two parts: first, Keynes's social philosophy, and second, the broad implications he drew for economic policy, above and beyond the need for active government intervention to achieve full employment. In the next chapter, we take up the relevance, in the light of our interpretation, of *The General Theory* for current economic policy.

SOCIAL PHILOSOPHY

In the 1920s, Keynes viewed himself as a man of the left: "I am sure I am less conservative in my inclinations than the average Labour voter. . . . The Republic of my imagination lies on the extreme left of celestial space."[2] In stating why he nevertheless could not join the Labour Party, Keynes divided that party into three wings: "the *Trade Unionists*, once the oppressed, now the tyrants, whose selfish and sectional interests need to be bravely opposed," "the *Communists*, who are committed by their creed to produce evil that good may come," and "the *Socialists*, who believe that the economic foundations of modern society are evil, yet might be good."[3] Keynes disdainfully rejected the aims and program of the *Trade Unionists* and the *Communists*. At the same time, he expressed sympathy with the aspirations of the *Socialists* though, to put it mildly, he was skeptical about the efficacy of the techniques they favored.

A decade before *The General Theory* he stated that "Constructive thinkers in the Labour Party and constructive thinkers in the Liberal Party [among whom he certainly included himself] are trying to replace them [the traditional socialist theories and programs] with something better and more serviceable. The notions on both sides are a bit foggy as yet,

---

[1]Keynes, "The End of Laissez-Faire," p. 294.
[2]Keynes, "Liberalism and Labor," pp. 308–9.
[3]Ibid., p. 309; Keynes's emphasis.

but there is much sympathy between them, and a similar tendency of ideas. I believe that the two sections will become more and more friends and colleagues in construction as time goes on."[4] Once Keynes put *The General Theory* together he believed he had found what these constructive thinkers had been seeking; he believed his theory made the traditional radical analysis and programs both obsolete and unnecessary; his new theory rendered obsolete the muddle that he felt Marxist economics to be.

In contrast to this sympathy with the ideals, if not the specifics, of the socialists, Keynes found the Conservatives anathema:

How could I bring myself to be a Conservative? They offer me neither food nor drink—neither intellectual nor spiritual consolation. I should not be amused or excited or edified. That which is common to the atmosphere, the mentality, the view of life of—well, I will not mention names—promotes neither my self-interest nor the public good. It leads nowhere; it satisfies no ideal; it conforms to no intellectual standard; it is not even safe, or calculated to preserve from spoilers that degree of civilization which we have already attained.[5]

In particular, he was not willing to give his all on the side of capitalism in a struggle against socialism:

. . . I think it would be for the health of the [Liberal] party if all those who believe . . . that the coming political struggle is best described as capitalism *versus* socialism, and thinking in these terms, mean to die in the last ditch for capitalism, were to leave us.[6]

The face he set upon his policy views prior to *The General Theory* can be characterized as a flirtation with a humane, decentralized socialism, a flirtation which was tempered by the discipline of an economist. He could not accept the mechanisms the socialists put forth to achieve their common goals.

To Keynes in 1926 the political problem was clear; it was

to combine three things: economic efficiency, social-justice, and individual liberty. The first needs criticism, precaution, and technical knowledge; the second, an unselfish and enthusiastic spirit that loves the ordinary man; the third, tolerance, breadth, appreciation of the excellencies of variety and independence, which prefers, above everything, to give unhindered opportunity to the exceptional and to the aspiring.[7]

[4] Ibid.
[5] Keynes, "Am I a Liberal?" pp. 296–97.
[6] Keynes, "Liberalism and Labor," p. 310.
[7] Ibid., p. 311.

In the last chapter of *The General Theory* Keynes returns to the triad of economic efficiency, social justice, and individual liberty. As far as economic efficiency is concerned, he argues that decentralized market processes do an adequate job in determining what is produced and how it is produced: "I see no reason to suppose that the existing system seriously misemploys the factors of production which are in use. . . . It is in determining the volume, not the direction, of actual employment that the existing system has broken down" (*GT*, p. 379); however, the market mechanism does fail in that it leads to a socially oppressive distribution of income and wealth. As will be argued later in this chapter in a discussion of the "euthanasia of the rentier," the determination of what is produced may be related to the distribution of income so that acceptance of the market mechanism as the determinant of the direction of employment may rest upon a prior short-circuiting of the market-determined distribution of income.

Social justice is best served by programs that guarantee an adequate volume of employment and a more fitting distribution of income and wealth. Efficiency and justice require that the socialization of investment necessary to assure full employment be combined with the elimination of the scarcity of capital, so as to achieve a marked reduction in income from capital, and direct (income and inheritance) taxation to achieve a proper income distribution.

So far as individual liberty is concerned, he argued that a system of individualism, by which he meant a decentralized market mechanism,

if it can be purged of its defects and its abuses, is the best safeguard of personal liberty in the sense that, compared with any other system, it greatly widens the field for the exercise of personal choice. It is also the best safeguard of the variety of life, which emerges precisely from this extended field of personal choice, and the loss of which is the greatest of all the losses of the homogeneous or totalitarian state. For this variety preserves the traditions which embody the most secure and successful choices of former generations; it colours the present with the diversification of its fancy; and, being the handmaid of experiment as well as of tradition and of fancy, it is the most powerful instrument to better the future. [*GT*, p. 380]

The three-pronged program, consisting of the socialization of investment, intervention to affect income distribution, and a decentralized market mechanism, was viewed as follows by Keynes:

Whilst, therefore, the enlargement of the functions of government, involved in

the task of adjusting to one another the propensity to consume and the inducement to invest, would seem to a nineteenth-century publicist or to a contemporary American financier to be a terrific encroachment on individualism, I defend
it, on the contrary, both as the only practicable means of avoiding the destruction of existing economic forms in their entirety and as the condition of the
successful functioning of individual initiative. [*GT*, p. 380]

Thus, Keynes chose capitalism, though not without considerable doubt
as to its virtues, and with the proviso that meaningful reforms be undertaken.

IMPLICATIONS FOR ECONOMIC POLICY

Introduction

Keynes was a political activist; he was always devising schemes and
programs. His view of the world was that

It is *not* true that individuals possess a prescriptive 'natural liberty' in their
economic activities. There is *no* 'compact' conferring perpetual rights on those
who have or on those who acquire. The world is *not* so governed from above that
private and social interest always coincide. It is *not* so managed here below that
in practice they coincide. It is *not* a correct deduction from the principles of
economics that enlightened self-interest always operates in the public interest.
Nor is it true that self-interest generally *is* enlightened, more often individuals
acting separately to promote their own ends are too ignorant or too weak to attain
even these.[8]

What was lacking in the inherited classical economics was a theory
which explained the operations of a capitalist economy in such a way
that the shortcomings of laissez-faire as a policy rule were made clear.
Such a theory would offer policy handles, i.e., operations, that men
imbued with a strong passion for social justice could urge and carry
through. The objective would be to so guide the economy that economic
efficiency could be a handmaiden of social justice and individual liberty.
The General Theory was Keynes's offering of such an analysis; the new
theory eliminated the need for thoroughgoing socialism, and it provided
the rationale and suggested the mechanism for efficient intervention in an
economy that remained basically capitalist.

In the final chapter of *The General Theory*, Keynes touches on three
broad policy questions—in addition to employment policy—to which the

[8]Keynes, "The End of Laissez-Faire," pp. 287–88.

argument is relevant. These are income distribution, the socialization of investment, and conflict among nations.

Income Distribution

Keynes begins his last chapter by asserting that:

> The outstanding faults of the economic society in which we live are its failure to provide for full employment and its arbitrary and inequitable distribution of wealth and incomes. The bearing of the foregoing theory on the first of these is obvious. But there are also two important respects in which it is relevant to the second. [*GT*, p. 372]

The General Theory's relevance to questions of income distribution is due to its refutation of the argument that income inequality is necessary to promote savings and to its pointing toward a regime in which, as a result of an epoch of full-employment accumulation, the scarcity of capital would be much reduced. Inasmuch as the rentier income from capital ownership reflects the scarcity of capital, full-employment accumulation, after a while, will lead to a sharp reduction of pure-capital income.

Keynes believed "that there is social and psychological justification for significant inequalities of incomes and wealth, but not for such large disparities as exist today" (*GT*, p. 374), and that the arguments which may legitimatize inequality in the distribution of incomes "do not apply equally to inequality of inheritances" (*GT*, p. 374).

One traditional and common argument for income inequality is that the well-to-do save a higher portion of their income than the poor, so that inequality, by raising the savings ratio, results in a larger share of output being available for the growth of capital. However, the new theory demonstrates that only in conditions of full employment is a low propensity to consume conducive to the growth of capital. In the absence of a guarantee that investment is always sufficient to assure that full employment rules, a low propensity to consume, by making full employment difficult to achieve, is an impediment to the growth of wealth:

> in contemporary conditions the growth of wealth, so far from being dependent on the abstinence of the rich, as is commonly supposed, is more likely to be impeded by it. One of the chief social justifications of great inequality of wealth is, therefore, removed. [*GT*, p. 373]

Keynes nevertheless believed both that "There are valuable human activities [mostly of an entrepreneurial nature] which require the motive of money-making and the environment of private wealth-ownership for their full fruition" (*GT*, p. 374) and that "dangerous human proclivities can be canalized into comparatively harmless channels by the existence of opportunities for money-making and private wealth" (*GT*, p. 374). On the other hand, "it is not necessary for the stimulation of these activities [useful money-grubbing] and the satisfaction of these proclivities [to dominate] that the game should be played for such high stakes as at present" (*GT*, p. 374). Thus, as "the task of transmuting human nature must not be confused with the task of managing it" (*GT*, p. 374), he held that "it may still be wise and prudent statesmanship to allow the game [of fortune making] to be played, subject to rules and limitations" (*GT*, p. 374). Keynes viewed the inequality of income that results from enterprise (mainly capital gains) as desirable, but the inequality of income that results from the "pure" ownership of wealth (the income of rentiers) as undesirable.

Keynes's view, therefore, was that moderate income differentials, smaller than the then-current and present differentials, were socially desirable, but that great income differentials—in particular those due to inheritance—were undesirable and unnecessary. Thus direct taxation of income and inheritance to ease the socially oppressive income distribution was desirable, and fortunately, as if by some invisible hand, such a modification of income distribution would also make the attainment and the sustaining of full employment easier.

Because of his economic theory and his view of the nature of human wants, Keynes believed that the amount of investment that would take place in a regime of continuous full employment, and in the absence of war and population growth, would soon lead to "the euthanasia of the rentier, and, consequently, the euthanasia of the cumulative oppressive power of the capitalist to exploit the scarcity-value of capital" (*GT*, p. 376).

He felt this euthanasia would occur because "the demand for capital is strictly limited in the sense that it would not be difficult to increase the stock of capital up to a point where its marginal efficiency had fallen to a very low figure" (*GT*, p. 375). Once the amount of capital is such that "*it ceases to be scarce,* so that the functionless investor will no longer receive a bonus" (*GT*, p. 376; emphasis added), then rentier income will cease. Combine this prognosis about the course of capital income with "a scheme of direct taxation, which allows the intelligence and determination and executive skill of the financier . . . to be harnessed to the service of the community on reasonable terms of reward" (*GT*, pp. 376–77), and an income distribution compatible with the triad of efficiency, justice, and liberty can be achieved.

Underlying Keynes's belief that capital could cease to be scarce was his view of the nature of human wants. Keynes was a young man during the Edwardian enlightenment, an optimistic era when the intellectual constraints and social hypocrisies of the Victorian era were being cast off, and genuine progress toward an egalitarian and open society seemed assured. In the Cambridge and London circles in which he traveled, human relations and affections were the central goods that were pursued. Lack of wealth, positon, and station was not a barrier to the achievement of true human satisfaction: affection, love, personal integrity, and human fulfillment were available to all. Keynes held that once the twin evils of abject grinding poverty and war were banished from the earth, not much more in the way of worldly goods than was within sight would be needed to achieve true affluence. True affluence could then be the lot of all regardless of their situation in life: for in the contemplated circumstances, the remaining modest differentials in private disposable income would not unduly constrain the attainment of true human satisfactions, even by the poorest.

Keynes approached the question of the ultimate required size of the capital stock with a view that human wants, *for those items that required substantial capital resources,* were satiable:

> Now it is true that the needs of human beings may seem to be insatiable. But they fall into two classes—those needs which are absolute in the sense that we feel them whatever the situation of our fellow human beings may be, and those which are relative in the sense that we feel them only if their satisfaction lifts us above, makes us feel superior to, our fellows. Needs of the second class, those which satisfy the desire for superiority, may indeed be insatiable; for the higher the general level, the higher still are they. But this is not so true of the absolute needs—a point may soon be reached, much sooner perhaps than we are all of us aware of, when these needs are satisfied in the sense that we prefer to devote our further energies to non-economic purposes.[9]

Keynes's view about the ability to satiate those human needs that require capital resources involves a circular argument; his personal standards and philosophy intrude into his argument. The universal satis-

---

[9]Keynes, "Economic Possibilities for Our Grandchildren," p. 326.

faction of the absolute needs for food, lodging, and other goods and services basic to life and health lies within the capacity of the affluent countries, such as the United States and Western Europe today (this objective was within or close to the technical capacity of these economies when Keynes was writing). The negative income tax and family allowance schemes which have been advanced recently show that the elimination of absolute poverty by modest transfer-payment schemes is fiscally feasible.

Nevertheless, in the presence of such present plenty with respect to "absolute" needs, capital continues to be scarce. In spite of the rapid accumulation since World War II, the scarcity of capital does not seem to be easing. Capital continues to command large positive return, and the euthanasia of the rentier seems to be nowhere in sight. One reason this is so is that what Keynes called the relative needs have grown, and the direction these relative needs have taken requires capital resources. Whereas Keynes contemplated in his 1930 essay on the "Economic Possibilities for Our Grandchildren" that the satiation of absolute needs would lead to a situation where "we prefer to devote our further energies to non-economic purposes," in fact, in the affluent societies, energies above those needed to satisfy the absolute needs have been devoted to the pursuit of relative needs that may, in their capital requirements, be even more capital-intensive than the traditional absolute needs.

Keynes's prediction that the rentier would wither away was based upon a generalization of his own preferences. We can speculate on why the world's preferences have turned in a direction which a civilized, humane, and, in a special way, equalitarian intellectual, whose standards were fixed during the Edwardian enlightenment, did not expect. One reason may be that the rich turned to consuming capital-intensive bundles of goods rather than philosophy and culture and that their example filtered down to the not so rich. Thus a variety of conspicuous consumption became generalized, and this conspicuous consumption has led to a continuing capital shortage. It is the income distribution associated with capital scarcity that may have set the consumption pattern that has led to the continuing capital shortage. In order to achieve the euthanasia of the rentier, it may be necessary to first achieve the income distribution that Keynes argued would exist after the euthanasia was achieved.

Furthermore, the direction taken by the growing relative needs is inspired by and largely the product of "education" in the guise of advertising. In our current system, affluence has not brought a demand for the quiet pleasures; but rather has been associated with proliferation of demands for goods that require capital assets. The generation of market positions that help augment capital scarcity has characterized the direction that private demand has taken in the period since Keynes.

Another reason why capital income has not withered away in the postwar period may lie in the structure of the government programs that have been developed to maintain full employment. In the pre–World War II emergency of the Great Depression, government programs designed to increase employment were heavily weighted toward the direct employment of labor. During World War II, a series of contractual devices for war production were developed which used private facilities for the manufacture of war material. In the postwar period, this contract system has been continued, both for the production of military equipment and in the production of more civilian-oriented goods. These contracts always provide for a substantial profit margin for the contractors. Not only has the postwar structure of policy designed to maintain income been heavily weighted toward the capital-consuming military needs, but the social structure of these policies has tended to subsidize capital income. Furthermore, inasmuch as the combination of military demand and the much larger schemes of transfer payments (social security, etc.) requires a heavy tax load, tax measures designed to aid capital income at the expense of consumers' income are available. In the generally conservative posture that postwar policy has taken, these available devices have been used.

It might well be that the euthanasia of the rentier in the form that Keynes envisaged it requires prior constraints on the growth of relative needs, and the constrained growth of relative needs requires an income distribution based on low or no income from capital ownership, i.e., the prior euthanasia of the rentier.

Underlying Keynes's vision of a world in which capital is no longer scarce is a world in which income distribution is such as to avoid encouraging ever more extravagant consumption, and in which "civilized" standards discipline and control relative needs and move consumption away from capital-intensive patterns. A world in which an endless accumulation of gadgetry and weaponry is the desire of man is not a world in which full investment will soon occur.

In addition to the need for disciplining and directing wants, Keynes held that there are two preconditions which had to be satisfied if the euthanasia of the rentier was to result from satiating the economy with capital: war was to be avoided and a stable population had to be attained. The preconditions have not been satisfied in the era since World War II. War destroys capital equipment. The seemingly endless arms race that has flowered since World War II is economically equivalent to war. Not only is the production of war material capital intensive, but the direction taken by the arms race, the development of ever more sophisticated weapons systems, regularly renders the capital equipment specialized to the production of displaced equipment obsolete. The succession of weapons systems has been equivalent to pillage and bombings in its destruction of the fruits of prior accumulation.

The decades following the Second World War saw a significant population expansion in the affluent countries (this may now be coming to a halt). The population boom led to a need for capital accumulation to furnish tools for the increasing population. Lower population growth, even in the presence of rapid technological change, should tend to lower the need to accumulate, and lead to a reduction in the rents capital can earn.

Keynes's vision that the euthanasia of the rentier, as a necessary outgrowth of the accumulation process, will radically decrease, if not eliminate, income from the ownership of scarce capital resources requires the prior achievement of a state of disciplined wants, a stable population, and a lifting of the burdens of war. None of these conditions have been fully satisfied—and of these conditions, it may well be that the disciplined-wants requirement is furthest from sight.

Keynes advanced two reasons why capital income should and would decrease as a proportion of total income. There was no need for high incomes to decrease the propensity to consume. In fact, a low propensity to consume is counterproductive, for it decreases the inducement to invest. Furthermore, in a short space of time, full investment could be achieved if full employment were maintained and if wants were disciplined. Once such full investment had been achieved then a new social order could emerge, for

All kinds of social customs and economic practices, affecting the distribution of wealth and of economic rewards and penalties, which we now maintain at all costs, however distasteful and unjust they may be in themselves, because they are tremendously useful in promoting the accumulation of capital, we shall then be free, at last, to discard.[10]

The Socialization of Investment

The General Theory was a product of the red thirties. With the Great Depression making the weaknesses of capitalism self-evident, thorough-going socialism was very prominent on the agenda of possible resolutions of the crisis. In contrast to complete socialism, Keynes held that "the foregoing theory is moderately conservative in its implications" (*GT*, p. 377). For once wise policy with respect to investment assures full employment, and wise policy with respect to direct taxation assures a reasonable income distribution, then socialism, in any thorough sense, is not necessary.

Keynes argued that there was "no reason to suppose that the existing system seriously misemploys the factors of production which are in use" (*GT*, p. 379), so that if the "central controls succeed in establishing an aggregate volume of output corresponding to full employment" (*GT*, p. 378) the market mechanism can be allowed full play. The central controls are to influence the aggregate propensity to consume and investment. Consumption can be influenced partly by a "scheme of taxation, partly by fixing the rate of interest, and partly, perhaps, in other ways" (*GT*, p. 378). The other ways presumably would include consumption financed by transfer payments, along with increased output of public goods.

However, as banking policy will be unable to induce sufficient investment for full employment at all times,

a somewhat comprehensive socialization of investment will prove the only means of securing an approximation to full employment though this need not exclude all manner of compromises and of devices by which public authority will co-operate with private initiative. But beyond this no obvious case is made out for a system of State Socialism which would embrace most of the economic life of the community. It is not the ownership of the instruments of production which it is important for the State to assume. If the State is able to determine the aggregate amount of resources devoted to augmenting the instruments and the basic reward of those who own them, it will have accomplished all that is necessary. Moreover, the necessary measures of socialization can be introduced gradually and without a break in the general tradition of society. [*GT*, p. 378]

[10]Ibid., p. 329.

Furthermore, once
central controls succeed in establishing an aggregate volume of output corresponding to full employment as nearly as is practicable, the classical theory
comes into its own again from this point onwards. If we suppose the volume of
output to be given, i.e. to be determined by forces outside the classical scheme of
thought, then there is no objection to be raised against the classical analysis of
the manner in which private self-interest will determine what in particular is
produced, in what proportions the factors of production will be combined to
produce it, and how the value of the final product will be distributed between
them. [*GT*, pp. 378–79]

There is an apparent inconsistency between Keynes's belief that it is
necessary to socialize investment to achieve full employment and the
view that the market does an acceptable job of allocating resources so
that private ownership and control can be retained. In part this inconsistency can be resolved if Keynes's views are put into the context of the
time they were stated and the then-current discussion. As mentioned
earlier, in the 1930s, with the world depression raging, socialism was
very much on the agenda. At the same time, civilized men were outraged
by Stalin's Russia; questions as to the inherent totalitarian bias of full-
blown socialism were being debated. In the early 1930s economists with
socialist sympathies were writing about market socialism and various
mixed systems in which the towering heights of the economy were
socialized while the rest of the economy remained private. Such market
or towering-heights socialisms are in principle consistent with Keynes's
perspective. These mixed-system resolutions of the problem of economic
organization would presumably be consistent with success in achieving
the twin goals of approximate full employment and the elimination or
radical reduction of private incomes from the ownership of wealth.

However, the socialist path was not taken as the Keynesian lessons
were assimilated and applied in the postwar period, even in countries
such as Britain, which had substantial periods of rule by nominally
socialist parties. The lesson that has been accepted, in part because
wartime policy succeeded in establishing full employment, is that a large
government sector, in part financed by deficits, can achieve and sustain
an approximation to full employment. The argument was developed and
accepted that there is no need to socialize ownership of industry. The
ownership of productive resources can be "safely" left in private hands,
as long as government, through its budget, is big enough. In the pro-

grams that were developed, the government expenditures necessary to sustain full employment took the form of claims upon productive capacity—building highways, paying for education and hospitals, arms, space adventures, etc.—and the form of transfer payments and subsidized consumption—social security, welfare, food stamps, medicare, etc.

This big government sector implied a large tax bite, so that the shape of tax schedules became a weapon for subsidizing (thus expanding) or taxing (thus constraining) various activities. As the gap between consumption at full employment, even allowing for transfer schemes, and full-employment output must be filled with either government spending that uses resources or private investment if full employment is to be sustained, measures to induce investment by increasing profitability have been insinuated into the tax and spending systems. Thus a high-profit, high-investment economy has been created in which tax and government-spending policies are evaluated on the basis of their impact upon private investment rather than on the basis of their impact upon consumption or equity with respect to income distribution. Full-employment policy has taken on a conservative coloration; what has been achieved might properly be called socialism for the rich.

However, as the tax schemes to induce investment bias income distribution in favor of the saving sectors, a treadmill process has developed in which ever-greater investment and ever-greater stimuli in the form of profits and subsidies to investment are needed to sustain full employment.

Thus the way the economy has developed is in marked contrast to the idea Keynes advocated, which was that if investment is inadequate to achieve full employment, then it is not desirable to induce a more rapid pace of investment by providing direct stimulants to private investment, but rather "measures for the redistribution of income in a way likely to raise the propensity to consume" (*GT*, p. 373) should be undertaken. In Keynes's view such consumption-oriented measures may in fact "prove positively favourable to the growth of capital" (*GT*, p. 373); government intervention, outside the socialized investment sector, is to be mainly directed at raising consumption propensities, primarily by policies that aim at achieving a more equitable distribution of income.

Conflict Among Nations

Keynes also believed that "if nations can learn to provide themselves with full employment by their domestic policy . . . there need be no important economic forces calculated to set the interest of one country against that of its neighbours" (GT, p. 382). Keynes viewed the tensions among the affluent nations of Europe and America as stemming from the felt needs to export in order to protect domestic employment, if not to raise domestic employment by "beggar my neighbor" policies.

For the first twenty-five years after the Second World War, this view of Keynes was borne out by relations among the affluent capitalist countries. Aside from vestiges of past colonialism, such as the Vietnam involvement by first France and then the United States, there was an absence of war and even of serious tensions among the countries that were both capitalist and affluent. The ideological Cold War is not a question of economic conflict. The ability to sustain domestic markets by monetary and fiscal policies eliminated pressures for countries to "compete" for controlled markets or advantageous positions in world trade.

Conclusion

Keynes believed that the policy implications of his theory were profound; not only did the theory point to ways in which a closer approximation to full employment can be sustained, but he envisaged that continuing full employment combined with an emphasis on consumption and public goods would lead to an egalitarian change in income distribution. The rentier income of the capitalist would disappear and the upper tail of the income distribution would be snipped off by taxation. He believed that both measures to raise the consumption function and the socialization of investment were necessary to sustain full employment and were desirable as social goals.

THE TWO LESSONS

As Keynes summarized The General Theory, he avowed that there were two lessons to be learned from the argument. The first was the obvious lesson that policy can establish a closer approximation to full employment than had, on the average, been achieved. The second, more subtle, lesson was that policy can establish a closer approximation to a more logical and equitable distribution of income than had been achieved.

To date the first lesson has been learned, albeit in a manner that makes an approximation to full employment heavily dependent upon government spending in the form of defense production and private investment that sacrifices present plenty for questionable benefits in the future. The economy has, for the time being, been controlled; the game that is economic life has been rigged so as to achieve a fair approximation to full employment. But in the development of policies to achieve full employment the second lesson has been forgotten; the need for policy aimed to achieve justice and equity in income distribution has not only been ignored but it has so to speak been turned on its head. What egalitarian bias existed in the tax schedules at the end of World War II has been attenuated.

Perhaps Keynes's famous statement that "the ideas of economists and political philosophers . . . are more powerful than is commonly understood. In fact the world is ruled by little else" (*GT*, p. 373) needs to be amended to allow the political process to select for influence those ideas which are attuned to the interests of the rich and the powerful. Certainly only one lesson from *The General Theory* has passed into the wisdom that guides policy. When conservatives are Keynesians, then tax and spending policies may well be used to give life to rentiers rather than to abet their euthanasia.

‹9›

Policy Implications of the Alternative Interpretation

During the first quarter-century after World War II the advanced capitalist economies succeeded in avoiding a great depression. For a while in the 1960s, self-proclaimed Keynesians were important government advisors and officials in the United States. They proclaimed the conquest of the business cycle as it was known in history. They asserted that by the appropriate use of monetary and fiscal policy, the economy could now be fine-tuned so that recessions and depressions would no longer take place.

According to the argument presented here, the model they used to analyze the economy and as a basis for determining appropriate policy maneuvers not only violated both the spirit and the substance of Keynes's *The General Theory* but also misspecified the economy they were dealing with. The model they used virtually ignored finance and uncertainty and thus was unable to introduce speculation in any meaningful sense as a proximate determinant of system behavior. Because of this misspecification their policy advice was based upon a model which implied that the dynamic processes of the economy led to steady growth rather than business cycles.

System behavior during the first half of the 1960s, when the economy steadily expanded, seemed to validate the claims of these advisors. The basic policy strategy of this period aimed at increasing private investment in order to induce a more rapid rate of growth. This strategy meant that policy's proximate aim was to achieve high, and rapidly increasing, profits. The steady expansion of the early 1960s and the tax and subsidy arrangements designed to induce investment, combined with the absence of a serious depression in the postwar period to date, set off a substantial investment boom in the mid-1960s. This investment boom was made possible by an increase in speculation with respect to liability structures by both financial and nonfinancial firms; speculation financed the expansion of total demand and most especially private investment.

As a result of the external financing of investment, the ratio of private debt payments to private incomes increased; this meant that payments due on liabilities became ever more closely articulated with cash receipts from various sources. In addition, liability management by financial institutions, households, and ordinary firms meant that an ever-increasing proportion of units became dependent upon the "normal" functioning of financial markets. The safety margins of receipts and liquid assets which provide for error and variance decreased. A robust financial system was transformed into a fragile system during the long expansion of the 1960s. As a result of the fragility, shocks that might well have been absorbed without serious repercussions in a more robust financial structure triggered incipient financial crises in the United States in 1966 and in 1969–70.

Prompt action by the Federal Reserve System in both 1966 and 1969–70 prevented these crises from setting off a full-scale debt-deflation process. However, the steps taken to abort a debt-deflation led to accelerated increases in the money supply. Because of these increases in the money supply and the basic fiscal posture of the government, the financial tensions resulted in only a pause in 1966 and a mild but somewhat persistent recession in 1970–71. The combination of the Federal Reserve's awareness of its financial responsibilities and the fiscal posture of the government has succeeded in changing the shape of the business cycle—the bottoms are not so low and recessions do not last as long—but it is now evident that the business cycle has not been banished by policy. It is also evident that the economy behaves quite differently with a fragile rather than a robust financial system and that the fragility of the financial system is related to the ratio of debt payments to operations income for the various sectors and the extent to which units are dependent upon refinancing their positions in long assets in smoothly functioning short-term financial markets.

Inflationary pressures on a sustained and accelerating basis first became evident in 1966 and have continued to date. In part these inflationary pressures are due to the manner in which the Federal Reserve is forced by threats of financial crises and debt-deflations to sustain a rapid increase in the money supply; in part they are due to the way in which money-wage rates are determined.

Keynesian analysis, most especially in the alternative formulation, is institutional, in the sense that actual behavior, which determines how the transition in which we spend our time develops, depends upon how the existing institutions behave. Thus our analysis allows the way in which money is created, investment is financed, and money wages are determined to affect the course of events. Within the alternative Keynesian model we have developed, if an accelerating pace of increases in money wages, especially wages of workers employed in the production of investment goods, is imposed upon the economy, if financial usages are such that the demand for investment financing will draw forth a supply of finances, if the Federal Reserve is constrained by the need to prevent crises and debt-deflations, and if the government's fiscal posture sets a high floor to employment, then prices will rise at the same accelerating pace as wages, if not faster because of the influence of anticipated increases. Whenever substantial unemployment for trade-union members is not a creditable possibility, trade unions become more powerful; and whenever past wage increases have been validated by subsequent price increases, employers become less resistant to further increases. The combination of protracted general prosperity, a low toleration for unemployment, and a fragile financial system is particularly conducive to accelerated inflation.

An inflationary process is especially likely to occur if trade unions are strong in the production of investment goods (construction) and full-employment policy is following an investment strategy. An increase in construction wages, by shifting the supply curve of investment output upward, forces the monetary and fiscal authorities to adjust their posture so that the demand price of investment goods rises with the supply price.

But the demand price of investment depends upon expected quasi-rents, and generalized inflation is necessary to increase quasi-rents across the board.

The power of rising wages in investment-goods production to force inflation on an economy dependent upon the external financing of investment is evident from the financing relations for investment. The internal financing capabilities of investing firms depend upon current quasi-rents, which in turn depend upon the current price level of output. If the supply price of investment goods increases due to wage increases of investment-goods workers, and if investment is sustained due to euphoric or inflationary expectations, then external finance has to make up the difference between the inflated costs and internal finance. Thus the increase in the required amount of external financing is greater than the rise in the price of investment goods suggests. For future quasi-rents from output in general to be high enough to generate sufficient cash to meet the enlarged future payment commitments embodied in the financial instruments that arise in such external financing of investment, the share of profits in income must increase, or the price level of output in general will follow the course set by the rise in construction wages. In an economy that approximates full employment, the possibility of increasing the share of profits in income is limited (unless tax or direct subsidies are increased). Beyond some point, increases in investment-goods wages will need to be fully reflected in current output prices (again unless subsidies are increased); if this does not happen, then either the investment strategy or the sustaining of full employment will have to be abandoned.

The events of the mid-1960s to date have validated the view we have attributed to Keynes that the availability of adequate finance is an essential step in generating and sustaining expansions. The investment boom of the 1960s together with the inventiveness of the financial system in discovering ways to accommodate the demand for finance constitute evidence that the endogenous generation of business cycles remains a basic characteristic of capitalist economies. Because of the efficacy of the Federal Reserve in aborting crises, and because of the high floor to income due to the size of the federal budget, no full-scale debt-deflation process has been triggered. Without a crisis and a debt-deflation process to offset beliefs in the success of speculative ventures, both an upward bias to prices and ever-higher financial layering are induced.

The active use of policy instruments following the guidelines drawn from the standard neoclassical model has succeeded in changing the shape of, even though it has not eliminated, the business cycle. Thus recent experience is consistent with the interpretation of Keynes's views that has been put forth here: we are dealing with a system that is inherently unstable, and the fundamental instability is "upward."

The economy is now a controlled rather than a laissez-faire economy; however, the thrust of the controls is not in the direction envisaged by Keynes. Investment has not been socialized. Instead, measures designed to induce private investment, quite independently of the social utility of investment, have permeated the tax and subsidy system. The strategy has not been to operate on the distribution of income so as to raise the consumption-income ratio; rather, the strategy has been to increase corporate untaxed income, which tends to lower the consumption-income ratio. (In 1929 the ratio of personal consumption expenditures to income in the United States was .75; in 1972 this same ratio was .63.) Further, the pattern of distribution of income has led to the proliferation of those relative needs that tend to sustain the scarcity of capital. The artificial stimulation via advertising of the consumption of things at the expense of what Keynes would have considered civilized standards, together with the waste of capital assets inherent in defense spending, has succeeded in fostering a continuing shortage of capital. Instead of taking the path Keynes advocated of first satisfying the absolute needs of all by raising minimal consumption standards and then turning to the pursuit of the important noneconomic goals of life, the high-investment strategy has the economy on a treadmill of ever-higher discretionary consumption, without any apparent tendency toward satiation. The joylessness of American affluence may be due to the lack of a goal, the acceptance of a standard in which "more" is really not worth the effort.

The success of a high-private-investment strategy depends upon the continued growth of relative needs to validate private investment. It also requires that policy be directed to maintain and increase the quasi-rents earned by capital—i.e., rentier and entrepreneurial income. But such high and increasing quasi-rents are particularly conducive to speculation, especially as these profits are presumably guaranteed by policy. The result is experimentation with liability structures that not only hypothecate increasing proportions of cash receipts but that also depend upon continuous refinancing of asset positions. A high-investment, high-profit strategy for full employment—even with the underpinning of an active fiscal policy and an aware Federal Reserve System—leads to an increasingly unstable financial system, and an increasingly unstable economic performance. Within a short span of time, the policy problem cycles among preventing a deep depression, getting a stagnant economy moving again, reining in an inflation, and offsetting a credit squeeze or crunch. Financial instability and business cycles, which were so evident historically, once again loom on the horizon. The apparent stability and robustness of the financial system of the 1950s and early 1960s can now be viewed as an accident of history, which was due to the financial residue of World War II following fast upon a great depression.

No economy, controlled or uncontrolled, can long survive as a free society unless it is deemed equitable, unless it is seen to promote social justice. The promotion of social justice by economic means requires that the inequalities of income correspond to some consensus as to the differential worth of the contributions made to the cooperative effort that produces income. In a highly interdependent urban economy, such a consensus cannot long be sustained unless inequality is constrained. Taxes and a distribution of the benefits of government intervention that are deemed to be fair or equitable are necessary for any economy, but especially for a controlled economy, to be robust. In a sense, the measures undertaken to prevent unemployment and sustain output "fix" the game that is economic life; if such a system is to survive, there must be a consensus that the game has not been unfairly fixed.

We are inevitably forced back to the normative question of for whom should the game be fixed and what kind of output should be produced. It is clear that if reasonably full employment is the dominant goal, then the scheme of perpetual waste and want has to date succeeded. The combination of investment that leads to no, or a minimal, net increment to useful capital, perennial war preparations, and consumption fads has succeeded in maintaining employment. But such a resolution of the problem of unemployment and depression does not lead a corresponding increase in felt well-being. It rather seems to put all—the affluent, the poor, and those in between—on a fruitless inflationary treadmill, accompanied by what is taken to be deterioration in the biological and social environment.

Furthermore, as high investment and high profits depend upon and induce speculation with respect to liability structures, the expansions become increasingly difficult to control; the choice seems to become whether to accomodate to an accelerating inflation or to induce a debt-deflation process that can lead to a serious depression. The success of the policy strategy based upon the view of how the economy functions that grew out of the standard interpretation of Keynes may be transitory. It truly is more difficult to set off a noninflationary, sustained expansion at present than it was a decade earlier, at the start of the 1960s.

During the Kennedy-Johnson years (1960–1968) a high-investment, high-profit, and military-spending strategy was formalized and applied, in part under the rubric of a policy for economic growth. An alternative is available in a high-consumption strategy. Once we recognize that under capitalist financial institutions, stability, especially an era of approximate full employment with accompanying notional growth, is destabilizing, then an appropriate strategy becomes to aim at decreasing the dependence of the system upon private investment—that is, to change income distribution so as to increase the average private propensity to consume, and accompany this with public consumption and investment.

An economy in which leading sectors are socialized, in which communal consumption satisfies a large proportion of private needs, in which taxation of income and wealth is designed to decrease inequality, and in which speculation in liability structures is limited by laws that determine permissible liability structures might well achieve a close approximation to sustained full employment without the tensions and instabilities that are inherent in the current policy strategy.

As socialization of the towering heights is fully compatible with a large, growing, and prosperous private sector, this high-consumption synthesis might well be conducive to greater freedom for entrepreneurial ability and daring than is our present structure. The high-investment, high-profits policy synthesis is associated with giant firms and giant financial institutions, for such an organization of finance and industry seemingly makes large-scale external finance easier to achieve. However, enterprises on the scale of the American giant firms tend to become stagnant and inefficient. A policy strategy that emphasizes high consumption, constraints upon income inequality, and limitations upon permissible liability structures, if wedded to an industrial-organization strategy that limits the power of institutionalized giant firms, should be more conducive to individual initiative and individual enterprises than is the current synthesis.

As it is now, without controls on how investment is to be financed and without a high-consumption, low-private-investment policy strategy, sustained full employment apparently leads to treadmill affluence, accelerating inflation, and recurring threats of financial crisis.

In the light of both the interpretation of Keynes we have advanced and recent experience it is apparent that there are limitations on how well a capitalist economy can do. The tendency for a capitalist economy to generate serious financial crises and business cycles remains, and the resolution of this tendency under existing arrangements seems to require continuous, if not accelerating inflation. However, the alternative interpretation indicates that with appropriate policy we can do better than we are now doing. To do better it is first necessary to constrain the liability structures of business firms. Debt-financing of investment and of positions in the stock of capital will have to be regulated, especially for large-scale organizations. In addition, the dependence upon a high rate of investment and upon government expenditures with no visible benefits, i.e., arms, must be reduced. Instead of a strategy in which the income of workers and the poor improves as a result of a "trickle downward" from growth of income of the affluent, an alternative strategy should be adopted in which the income of the poor is sustained and increased directly, and the affluent take their chances.

As was mentioned earlier, because the financial repercussions of a high-investment, high-profit strategy are destabilizing, the success that the current strategy has enjoyed to date may prove to be transitory. If this is true and if reasonable full employment is to be sustained then the alternative approach that has been sketched, which emphasizes egalitarian income distribution and high consumption, will be a feasible alternative strategy compatible with economic efficiency, social justice, and individual liberty. If we take a longer philosophical perspective, we might contemplate a succession of eras in which different full-employment income-distribution strategies are appropriate; a high-investment, high-profit regime might well be succeeded by a high-consumption, egalitarian regime, and then back again. It will remain true that we live out our lives in transition; there is no final solution to the problems of organizing economic life.

The revolution in economic theory and policy that Keynes believed he was fathering was aborted in two ways. The revolution in theory was reduced to a static equilibrium analysis and then assimilated with the classical doctrines. The objective of the revolution in policy was to achieve the goals of socialists without the statism and homogeneity which he believed followed from their muddled, even obsolete, analysis and policy prescriptions. As it has been interpreted, Keynes's theory does not provide the basis for a new and rational radical doctrine. The standard interpretation makes Keynes the apostle of a new conservatism that promotes investment at the expense of private and public consumption and income inequality at the expense of social justice.

Thus in order to arrive at a satisfactory analysis of how a capitalist economy of the 1970s functions, it is necessary to go back to and understand the problems that confronted economists in the 1930s, the period when *The General Theory* was developed. In a similar matter, in order to understand the policy issues confronting advanced capitalist countries today it is necessary to return to the issues that were central to the fundamental debate that took place in the 1930s on the relative merits of capitalism and socialism. If one comes down, as Keynes did, on the side of a mixture that sustains the basic properties of capitalism, it is not because of the virtues of unconstrained capitalism but rather in spite of its defects, which, though great, can in principle be controlled. But if capitalism is to be controlled so that the basic triad of efficiency, justice, and liberty is achieved, then the design of the controls will have to be enlightened by an awareness of what was obvious to Keynes—that with regard to both the stability of employment and the distribution of income, capitalism is flawed.

Bibliography

Ackley, Gardner. *Macroeconomic Theory*. New York: Macmillan, 1961.

Clower, R. W. "Foundations of Monetary Theory," in *Monetary Theory*. Baltimore, Maryland: Penguin Books, 1969; Chapter 14.

Fisher, Irving. "The Debt-Deflation Theory of Great Depressions," *Econometrica*, 1(1933), pp. 337–57.

Galbraith, John Kenneth. "How Keynes Came to America" in *Economics, Peace, and Laughter*. New York: New American Library, 1972; pp. 44–56.

Hahn, F. H. *On the Notion of Equilibrium in Economics*. Cambridge, England: Cambridge University Press, 1973.

Hansen, Alvin. *Monetary Theory and Fiscal Policy*. New York: McGraw-Hill, 1949.

Harrod, Ray Forbes. *The Life of John Maynard Keynes*. New York: Harcourt, Brace & World, 1951.

Hicks, J. R. "Mr. Keynes and the 'Classics'; A Suggested Interpretation," *Econometrica*, 5(1937), pp. 147–59.

Keynes, J. M. "Alternative Theories of the Rate of Interest," *Economic Journal*, 47 (June 1937), 241–52.

———. *The Collected Writings of John Maynard Keynes*. 28 vols. London and Basingstoke: Macmillan, for the Royal Economic Society, 1973.

Keynes, J. M. *Essays in Persuasion*. Vol. 9 of *The Collected Writings of John Maynard Keynes*. Contains:
"Am I a Liberal?" pp. 295–306;
"Can Lloyd George Do It?" pp. 86–125;
"The Consequences to the Banks of the Collapse of Money Value," pp. 150–58;
"The Economic Consequences of Mr. Churchill," pp. 244–70;
"Economic Possibilities for Our Grandchildren," pp. 321–32;
"The End of Laissez-Faire," pp. 272–94;
"Liberalism and Labor," pp. 307–11.

—— . "The 'Ex-Ante' Theory of the Rate of Interest," *Economic Journal*, 47 (December 1937), 663–69.

—— . "The General Theory of Employment," *Quarterly Journal of Economics*, 51 (February 1937), 209–23.

—— . *The General Theory of Employment, Interest, and Money*. New York: Harcourt, Brace, 1936; reprinted as vol. 7 of *The Collected Writings of John Maynard Keynes*. (Note: Most editions follow the pagination of this one.)

—— . "Recent Economic Events in India," *Economic Journal*, 19 (March 1909), 51–67.

—— . "The Theory of the Rate of Interest," in *Readings in the Theory of Income Distribution*, vol. 3. Philadelphia: Blakiston, 1946; pp. 418–24.

—— . *A Treatise on Money*. New York: Harcourt, Brace, 1930.

—— . *A Treatise on Probability*. Vol. 8 of *The Collected Writings of John Maynard Keynes*.

Leontief, Wassily W. "The Fundamental Assumption of Mr. Keynes' Monetary Theory of Unemployment," *Quarterly Journal of Economics*, 51(November 1936), 147–67.

Minsky, H. P. "Monetary Systems and Accelerator Models," *American Economic Review*, 47 (December 1957), 859–83.

Patinkin, Don. *Money, Interest, and Prices: An Integration of Monetary and Value Theory*. 2d. ed. New York: Harper & Row, 1965.

Phillips, A. W. "The Relation between Unemployment and the Rate of Money Wage Rates in the United Kingdom, 1862–1957," *Economica*, 1958.

Robertson, D. H. *Banking Policy and the Price Level: An Essay in the Theory of the Trade Cycle*. London: P. S. King & Son, 1926.

Robinson, Joan. *Economic Heresies*. New York: Basic Books, 1971.

Simons, Henry Calvert. *Economic Policy for a Free Society*. Chicago: University of Chicago Press, 1948.

Sweezy, Paul M. "John Maynard Keynes," in *Keynes' General Theory: Reports of Three Decades*, ed. Robert Lekachman. New York: St. Martin's Press, 1964.

Viner, Jacob. "Mr. Keynes on the Causes of Unemployment," *Quarterly Journal of Economics*. 51(November 1936), 147–67.

Index